Travels in Brittany

Dinan

Travels in Brittany

Mary Elsy
with
Jill Norman

MEREHURST PRESS
LONDON

Published in 1988 by Merehurst Press
5 Gt. James Street
London, WC1N 3DA

Co-Published in Australia and New Zealand by
Child and Associates
5 Skyline Place, French's Forest
Sydney 2086,
Australia

ISBN 1 85391 002 3

Printed in Great Britain by Hartnolls Limited

Typeset by Maggie Spooner Typesetting
Designed and produced by Snap! Books
Illustrations by Beatrix Blake
Cover illustration by Beatrix Blake
Maps by Sue Lawes

Contents

Château de Combourg

Introduction
to
Brittany

How to Use this Book

In the central section of *Travels in Brittany* there is a detailed itinerary of an 11-day tour of the region. The route chosen circles the area beginning and ending at St-Malo (see p. 30-1 for details). In the final part of the book there are sample menus and recipes to bring the techniques of Breton cuisine home with you. This introductory section offers a selection of background information on Brittany to assist you on your travels.

Religion

'The Bretons,' say the French, 'fear God and the sea and naught else in the universe.' Even their moods — gloomy or boisterous — reflect the sea. They are fierce fighters with tempers like the storms which smash against their cliffs. Hell in Breton legend is a world of ice, rain, mists and fog in which lost souls eternally wander, rather than a fiery furnace. Ankou, the Lord of the mysterious other world, is generally represented as a skeleton, armed with a pitchfork, usually veiled in a shroud, who sails along the coast in a barque or drives along a country lane in a chariot. No one who sees him will remain alive for long.

This imaginative and deeply religious people cling more closely to their old beliefs than their more rational French neighbours. Each village has its own special saint, many of whom have never been heard of anywhere else. Mystic and joyous festivals, called *pardons*, are held all over Brittany in honour of a saint of a particular chapel or hamlet. The name comes from the churches' custom of granting indulgences to pardon people's sins on a Saint Day. The faithful also come to fulfil a vow or beg for grace. A legend is usually wound about the pardon of one of these places. The great pardons are most impressive and it is well worth organising your trip to Brittany so that one can be fitted in. Old Breton costumes will be worn in a spectacular procession. Candles, banners and statues of saints are borne aloft by singing people, accompanied by priests and probably several Bishops. An ordinary fair is held afterwards.

Brittany does not possess as many fine churches, cathedrals and châteaux as neighbouring Normandy. This was due to her poverty, long periods of internal strife and the use of local granite, which is hard and difficult to work.

Because the construction of large churches and cathedrals were usually held up by lack of money, they took centuries to complete and thus incorporated a number of different styles. The best cathedrals are to be found at St-Pol-de-Léon, Tréguier, Quimper, Nantes and Dol-en-Bretagne. Belfries, usually square, symbolic of both religious and civil life, were greatly prized, as were the porches often decorated with the figures of the apostles, where the parish notables gathered. You will also see many fountains, especially in lower Brittany. Most of them, under the protection of a saint, were sacred and were used by pilgrims at pardons.

Breton craftsmen, inspired by strong religious feelings, put a great deal of energy into the wood and stone decorations of their parish churches (especially from the 15th to the 18th centuries), which were usually very large. You will notice many fine choir and rood screens, baptismal fonts, pulpits, altarpieces, triptyches, also stained-glass windows, and gold plate. These were generally made by local craftsmen.

The parish closes, which were mostly built during the 17th century, are a typical Breton feature. They comprise a cemetery (the community's spiritual life is always closely linked with the dead), reached by a triumphal arch, an ossuary (now usually a chapel) and a calvary (a teaching device, an elaborate monument, showing episodes from the Passion surrounding Christ on the cross). Calvaries were also supposed to help ward off the plague: they were sometimes set up as a thanksgiving for one that had ended.

History

For centuries forests and rough country isolated the Brittany peninsula from the mainland of France. Little is known about its earliest inhabitants, except that they were a Mediterranean people. In southern Brittany, they appear to have been prosperous traders in tin and copper, and have left behind remains of their culture in the shape of megaliths — menhirs (long stones), dolmens (stone tables) and cromlechs (circles of standing stones), probably all connected in some way with sun-worship. The Celts, who arrived in the country about the 6th century BC, most likely intermarried with these previous inhabitants. They divided the land up between five tribes.

After the defeat of the powerful Veneti in southern Brittany by the Romans in 56 BC, Brittany was added to the Roman Empire. However although customs and language were Romanised, roads built and agricultural estates founded, its Romanisation was largely superficial. Indeed, Christianity did not take much hold until the 4th century. It mainly arrived later with the next wave of invaders, fellow Celts from Britain, who left their country, perhaps driven by the Scots, Angles and Saxons, and settled in Brittany during the 5th and 6th centuries AD, giving it its name, 'Little Britain' or 'Brittany'. The missionaries, who came with them, chiefly from Ireland and Wales, are now regarded as saints, and many Breton towns and villages were named after them. Some of the pagan menhirs were crowned with a cross.

Brittany became a province of the Frankish empire, and was divided into a loosely-knit, petty lordship until a Breton hero, Count Nominoë of Vannes, managed to throw off Frankish suzerainty and defeated the French king, Charles the Bald, near Redon. His independent dynasty, founded in 845, lasted more than one hundred years.

Brittany retained its links with Britain which helped to revive the region. However, later Norman invasions forced many Bretons to flee their homes. Although Alain Barbe-Torte (crooked beard) the young Breton heir, returned from his sanctuary at the English court to expel the Norman invaders, this warfare strengthened the Breton nobles and weakened his dynasty. The resulting strife and poverty lasted until the end of the 14th century.

Brittany, fiercely jealous of her independence, kept the French king at bay until Philippe-Auguste managed to bring the governship of the province into French hands. But when the line of French-sponsored dukes ruling from Rennes ended on the death of the childless John III in 1341, the resulting War of Succession (1341–1364) brought England and France into open conflict. Charles de Blois, married to John III's niece, Jeanne de Penthièvre, was supported by the English Edward III. Brittany was brought to near ruin before Charles de Blois was defeated at the battle of Auray, and John's son became John IV. Fortunately, he and the next five dukes proved good rulers. The restored duchy entered upon a prosperous and golden period.

François II, the sixth duke, continuing the policy of maintaining Brittany's

11

independence, allied himself with England, and even tried to fix up a marriage between his daughter and the Prince of Wales. Anne, trying to maintain her country's independence from France, allied herself with Maximillian of Austria. But after her father's defeat by the French king at St-Aubin-du-Cormier in 1488, and his later death, she was eventually obliged to marry first Charles VII of France, then Louis XII. Anne, a staunch Catholic, devoted administrator and patroness of the Arts, has always held a high place in Breton history. She did her best to preserve Breton autonomy by marrying her daughter, Claude, to Maximillian's grandson, the future Charles V, but in the end Claude was betrothed to her cousin François d'Angoulême, the future François of France. Claude later ceded the duchy to their son, the Dauphin. In 1532, the States (Council) meeting at Vannes proclaimed Brittany's union with the kingdom and crown of France, although the province was allowed to retain many of its old rights and privileges.

Much fighting took place in Brittany during the Wars of Religion. The Duke of Mercoeur, a governor of Brittany, tried to take advantage of the anarchic situation to increase his own powers. Peace came to the province when Protestant Henri IV, converted to Catholicism, signed the Edict of Nantes in the ducal castle there in 1598.

At first, Brittany welcomed the Revolution. There had been risings over an unpopular tax on tobacco, pewter, vessels and stamps in 1675 and riots over attacks on their privileges in 1719. The peasantry were discontented with their poor living conditions and the middle class dissatisfied with their status. Later, they resented attacks on their special rights and were disgusted by the Revolution's excesses, particularly the execution of the king, Louis XVI, and the drowning of 13,000 political prisoners in the Loire, below Nantes.

Enforced conscription, interference with her trade privileges, and the persecution of her priests, caused many Bretons to join the Chouans (a name given to bands of peasants, also smugglers, who used the hoot of an owl at night as their secret signal), and the Vendéen royalists. The Chouans were defeated after the ill-fated British-backed landings at Quiberon Bay in 1795 and the execution of the Vendéen leaders ended the struggle, although subsequent risings took place in 1799, 1815 and even in 1832 in the nearby Vendée.

Napoleon completed the work of centralisation. The Breton language was forbidden in the new colleges and lycées. But Brittany was still politically suspect and regarded as a backward, rather dangerous if picturesque region. New life was brought to some of the coastal towns by the introduction of canning, particularly sardine and tunny. Much of the cereal-growing region was devoted to wheat, and potatoes were widely cultivated. Market-gardens and cider production contributed to the wealth of the 'golden belt' (warmed by the gulf stream), the coast between St-Malo and the Loire. But lack of industrialisation and an increased population lead to widespread un-employment. From the middle of the 19th century there were about one and a quarter million Bretons spread around the world. Many went to Paris to work as domestic-servants, labourers and artisans.

This individualistic region lost many soldiers and sailors in the First World War: in the Second, it contributed more men than any other province in France to the Free French Forces Resistance movement. Some of the last war's fiercest fighting took place in Brittany. Ports such as Brest, Lorient and St-Nazaire and St-Malo were devastated.

To some extent Chouanism has lingered on in the form of Breton nationalism. Manifestations of this appeared in the last war — Hitler played on Brittany's separatist leanings. More recently, there has been a revival of the teaching of Breton in public schools, the flying of the black and white national flag in public places (it consists of five black bands, which symbolise the Bishoprics of Haute Bretagne and four white bands representing those of Basse Bretagne while the nine ermines in the top left corner date back to the emblem of the old duchy), multiplying folk-groups, a number of Breton poets, and, alas, the occasional blowing up of French government buildings.

Geography and Industry

Brittany has the greatest geographical and homogeneous unity of any region in France; it is divided into four departments, Ille-et-Vilaine, Côtes-du-Nord, Finistère and Morbihan. Except for Loire-Atlantique, which is now incorporated into Pays-de-la-Loire outside Brittany, these divisions are much the same as those made when the region was divided up between the original five Celtic tribes. Physically Brittany divides into two main regions — High Brittany in the east and Low Brittany in the west. These names are odd in that High Brittany is chiefly low-lying, while Low Brittany is hilly! Low Brittany, the *Bretagne Bretonnonte* is more remote and one is more likely to find old Breton customs and hear Breton spoken there.

Brittany's attraction today, as always, is the sea coast. Its name, 'the Armor', the country near the sea, was given to this region by the Gauls. Its extreme indentation, or saw-teeth, make the length of its coastline something like 750 miles. Add to this the islands, islets and reefs. Brittany's best seascapes are at its western end. Here some local names have a sinister if superstitious ring, such as Baie des Trépassés (Bay of the Dead) and Enfer de Plogoff (the Hell of Plogoff). Then there are the pink granite statuary of Ploumanach and Trégastel, the cave of Morgat, and the grand promontory of Cap Fréhel. There are wide sandy beaches and harsh rugged points made barren by salty sea winds, and sheltered bays where the climate is so mild that hot-house plants such as mimosas, agaves, palms and fig trees flourish.

Brittany's climate is oceanic. The north is cooler than the south, and the west than the east; it is also wetter. Over a metre of rain a year is usual in the hillier regions, but this ensures that all the rivers are amply supplied and flow well. The mild winters, foliowed by temperate springs, make early vegetables of prime agricultural importance, especially in the sheltered areas along the coast, and near the mouth of the Loire. Some fruit, especially strawberries and, of course, apples for the delicious cider, are also grown.

But obviously the main produce of Brittany comes from the sea. Inland fishing takes place all along the coast while deep-sea trawlers operate in the Bay of Biscay, the Irish Sea and off Iceland. Crustacean fishing mostly takes place along the coast but some lobster boats go as far as Mauretania. Brittany has long been an important region for flat oysters (bélons). Algae and seaweed are harvested and used as fertiliser. Half the ships in France are produced in Brittany — merchant ships at St-Nazaire and naval at Brest and Lorient.

Inland, the 'Argoat' (country of the woods) is fairly uniform, a land of rolling hills and valleys, but never mountainous. The highest peak in the country's spine, the Arrée 'mountains', is about 1200 feet and in the Noires 'mountains', 1043 feet. Brittany is one of France's foremost agricultural regions, producing 20% of French dairy products, and is also an important pig-producing region. Industry is most active in central Brittany, especially around Rennes.

The construction of roads, railways and canals over the last hundred years, the Common Market and economic and regional planning have also helped Brittany to become more prosperous and outward looking. Her industries are diverse and scattered — shipbuilding, building, engineering and mining (kaolin, slate, tin), canning (natural outlet for local products), algae-processing plants, paper-making and tanning. There are also many small local industries, for instance the famous pottery works at Quimper and cidermaking carried out by both individual farms and larger combined establishments.

Tourism is probably today's greatest money-spinner. Brittany is especially ideal for family holidays. One can find anything from simple to top-class accommodation. Villas, cottages and flats may be hired. There are many well-equipped camp-sites. The indented coast line, with so many sheltered bays and islands offering safe anchorage, make it popular among those with sailing and motor crafts, also sailing clubs (such as at Glénan). One can travel from the channel to the Atlantic coast by canal boat.

Public transport is not very good in Brittany. The coast is served by rail, the interior mainly by local buses (they are not numerous, you will need a lot of patience). To explore the region properly a car is necessary. Bikes may be hired for exploring the immediate surroundings.

Seaside cures or thalassotherapy (use of sea water and sometimes seaweed) attract those suffering from rheumatism and arthritis. There are centres at St-Malo, Carnac, Quiberon, Perros-Guirec and Roscoff.

Famous Names

As with Normandy, learning in Brittany was centred in the monasteries. Latin was the language used, and subjects studied were mostly concerned with the Breton church, moral philosophy and the lives of the saints.

Perhaps the most renowned of the thinkers was Peter Abélard (1079–1142) born at Pallet, near Nantes, the eldest son of a Breton lord. He became a scholar in Paris and, at the age of 22, a teacher and later a Professor of

15

Theology. Students flocked to his lectures and his books (hand-written) were read by many. His opinion that no belief should be accepted unless it could be proved made him many enemies in the superstitious church of that time. After his romantic love affair with the beautiful and accomplished Héloise, with whom he was unhappily obliged to part, he became the Abbot of St-Gildas-de-Rhuys. He was soon disillusioned with its backwardness. 'I see only savages . . . my monks here have only one rule, which is to have none at all . . . I always seem to see a sword hanging over my head,' he wrote to Héloise. The monks used poison to try and rid themselves of this enlightened abbot. He survived to escape via a secret passage in 1140.

Perhaps one should mention the medieval *La Matière de Bretagne* (the Matter of Brittany) a collective title given to works inspired by Celtic mythology, especially the Arthurian legend, which has fascinated so many people. King Arthur was the legendary British chieftain who helped to defend his country against Saxon invaders. Geoffrey of Monmouth's 12th-century *History of the Kings of Britain*, which was later translated into French, turned Arthur into a powerful and cultured sovereign, surrounded by valiant knights. These romances, set in Britain, Ireland and Armorica, had an influence on the 'Chanson de geste' (song about a heroic deed) and the literature of chivalry. Although Britain played a leading role in the *Matter of Brittany*, the Armoricans contributed to the general culture through their lays (poems sung by harpists) and the legends that inspired many 12th- and 13th-century troubadours and writers. Although these were scorned during the Renaissance and ignored during the 17th and 18th centuries, they were rediscovered by the Romantics. A journey to Brittany became a 'must' for many distinguished 19th-century writers, such as Balzac, Flaubert, Stendhal, Hugo, George Sands, Maupassant and Proust. The surrealist Guillaume Apollinaire wrote poems about the wizard Merlin.

After a university was founded in Nantes in the 15th century, students went there to study. Two well-known figures in the 17th and 18th centuries were Madame de Sévigné and Alain-René Lesage. Madame de Sévigné (1626–1696) left a widow at 25, devoted her life to her children, the care of her country estates and an active cultural social life from which she excluded fresh emotional attachments. Her letters, of which 1500 survive, were written mostly between 1664 and 1696 to friends and relations but mostly to her daughter, Françoise-Marguerite, who became the Countess of Grignan, and lived in Provence. She wrote of the day-to-day happenings, in Paris and Versailles, and about her quiet life at Les Richers, her estate in Brittany, where she often stayed. She had a sharp eye for detail, could be malicious and gave her own vivid impressionistic view of contemporary history. Alain-René Lesage (1668–1747) from Vannes, a contemporary of Defoe and whose works influenced Smollet, was one of the first French novelists. He used the 'portrait' and 'character' in such a way as to blend into the narrative and so was amongst the creators of the modern novel. His best work was *Gil Blas de Santillane* (1715–1735).

Brittany's three best-known 19th-century writers were Chateaubriand, Lamenais and Renan. François René de Chateaubriand (1768–1848) was the tenth and last child of a noble Breton family who had fallen on hard times. His father set up as a shipowner in St-Malo. Chateaubriand a romantic, torn between entering the priesthood and going to sea, fought for the emigré army, went to England and America, became a diplomat under Napoleon (but found his politics too tyrannical), and later served under the Bourbon restoration. He retired from public life in 1830. Two of his major works were *La Vie de Rancé* (1844), the biography of a 17th-century priest whose life Chateaubriand believed reflected his own, and *Mémoires d'Outre-Tombe* (1848), written to be published after his death. Ernest Renan (1823–1892) born at Tréguier, was a candidate for the priesthood but religious doubts turned his thoughts towards science. His chief interest, though, lay in the history of religion. His principal work was *Histoire des Origines du Christianisme* (1863–1881). He described his native Brittany in *Souvenirs d'Enfance et de Jeunesse* (1883).

Anatole Le Braz (1859–1926) a celebrated Breton folklorist should perhaps also be noted and certainly Jules Verne (1828–1905) born at Nantes, a harbinger of modern science-fiction. His tales were based on scientific concepts, unknown then, but which were often later realised. One story *The Nautilus* anticipated the submarine. Most of his books (unlike those of other Breton writers) have been translated into English. Pierre Loti (1850–1923), a naval officer by profession, based his novels on personal experience, mostly love-affairs which ended unhappily in a parting, set against an exotic foreign background.

It is difficult to find any significant Breton painters. Artistic talent seems to have been directed into stone sculpture — Michel Colombe (1431–1512) was a native of St-Pol-de-Léon — or into wood-carving, and decorating rood screens, rood beams, fonts, pulpits and altar-pieces, or painting stained-glass windows and making gold church-plate.

However, Brittany did attract artists to work there, such as at Pont-Aven, where Paul Gauguin (1848–1903) went to paint. The earliest of his most characteristic pictures were painted there in 1888. His picture 'Jacob wrestling with the Angel' depicts how this biblical episode might appear to Breton peasant women after it had been described to them in a sermon. Gauguin organised an exhibition of the painters who had worked with him in Brittany at Café Volpini in Paris. His followers called themselves the 'Nabis' (the Hebrew word for prophet).

The Epicure's Guide

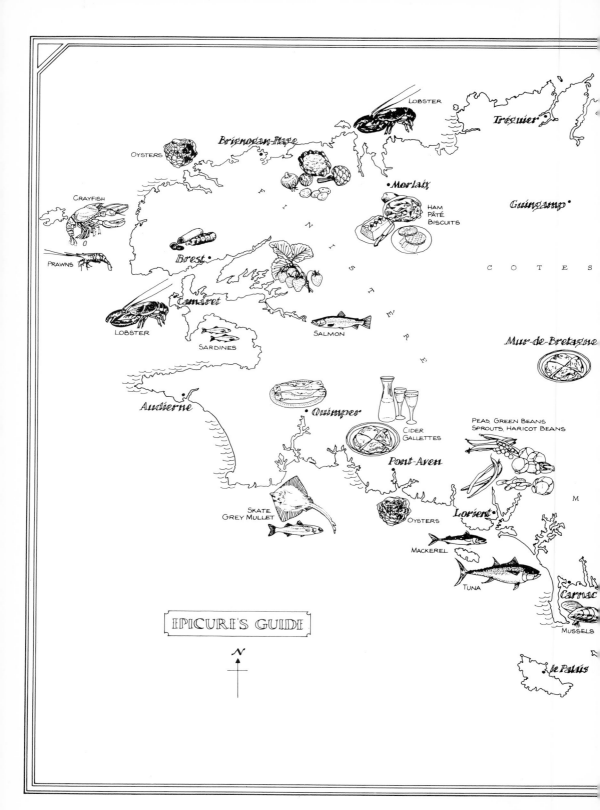

Lobster

Tréguier

Brignogan-Plage

Oysters

Guingamp

Morlaix

Crayfish

HAM
PÂTÉ
BISCUITS

F
I
N
I
S
T
È
R
E

Brest

COTES

Prawns

Camaret

Mur-de-Bretagne

Lobster

Salmon

Sardines

M

Audierne

Quimper

CIDER
GALLETTES

PEAS, GREEN BEANS
SPROUTS, HARICOT BEANS

Pont-Aven

Skate
Grey Mullet

Oysters

Lorient

M

Mackerel

Carnac

Tuna

Mussels

EPICURE'S GUIDE

le Palais

N

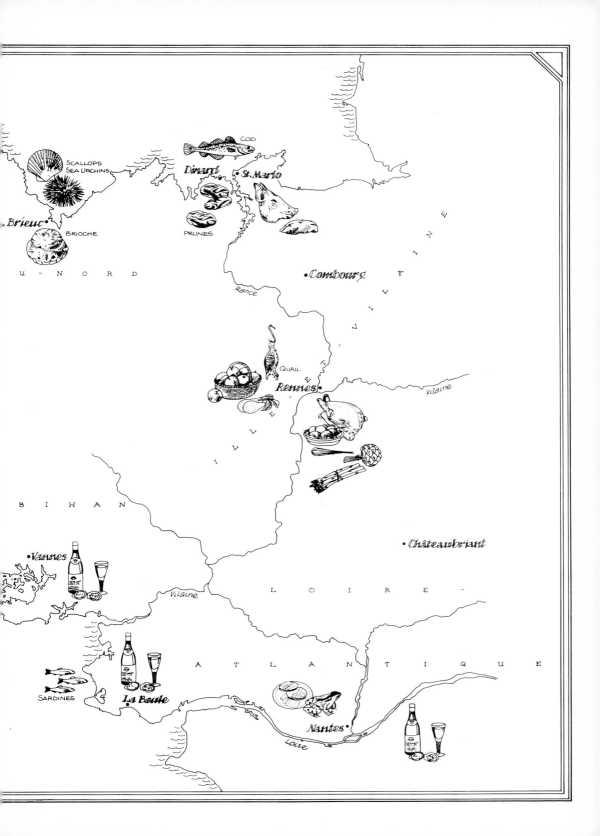

SCALLOPS
SEA URCHINS

COD

Dinard

St. Malo

• Brieuc •

BRIOCHE

PRUNES

U - N O R D

Rance

• Combourg

QUAIL

Rennes •

Vilaine

B I H A N

• Vannes

• Châteaubriant

Vilaine

L O I R E -

A T L A N T I Q U E

SARDINES

La Baule

Nantes •

Loire

Food

Brittany may have few famous local dishes but the province certainly produces excellent raw materials. It is a paradise for lovers of fish and seafood; its vegetables and fruits — notably strawberries — are superb and it produces most of France's best pork and chickens.

The food tends to be simple, hardy and sustaining as befits this rugged peninsula jutting out into the Atlantic. In culinary terms Brittany divides neatly into two regions, Haute-Bretagne to the north, along the English Channel coast, which is influenced by Norman cider and cream-based cooking, and Basse-Bretagne which extends from the Atlantic coast down to the Loire Valley and uses the light Muscadet wines in its dishes.

Armor, the land of the sea, is the Breton name for the beautiful coastline, and the further west you travel towards the Atlantic the more windswept and craggy the landscape becomes. For centuries here the men gathered shellfish and went fishing when the lashing seas permitted, whilst the women cultivated the land, growing potatoes and reliable grain crops like barley, rye and oats — the same crops as in the other Celtic countries, Wales, Scotland and Ireland. Buckwheat, which is not in fact a grain, was introduced later on because it grows well in poor soil.

Inland is Argoat, the land of the woods, a reference to the great forests of the past, for although some pockets of woodland survive, this is essentially farming country today. The inland region was very little influenced by the coast in the past; vegetables and grains were once again the principal crops, and the pig replaced fish as the occasional item of flesh in the diet.

Hardy grains do not contain sufficient gluten to be made into breads successfully, so the Bretons made them into porridge called bouillie. Thicker porridges blended with a little fat were wrapped in cloths and boiled to make puddings called fars. The far of Brittany is an ancient dish, exactly the same as the staple food eaten by the seafaring Phoenicians five thousand years ago and perhaps brought to Brittany by those traders, for there is no evidence that far travelled overland — porridge was known throughout southern and central Europe but not far pudding.

Far is still very much a part of the Breton diet, although in the last sixty or seventy years it has undergone many transformations with the addition of sugar, honey, cream and flavourings. Contemporary recipes for far are still based on buckwheat flour but then include eggs, milk, cream, melted butter, sugar and dried fruit in varying proportions. The pudding is still boiled in a cloth or a coarse linen bag (then called far-en-sac). One of the most common ways to cook it in the region of Léon, around Roscoff, is in a pot-au-feu called kig-ha-farz in Breton. A hearty stew is made with salted belly pork, maybe some sausages or a piece of ox tail and vegetables — onions, leeks, carrots, cabbage. The stew is simmered for several hours and the pudding in its bag is added towards the end. To serve kig-ha-farz, the meat is sliced and put on a platter with the vegetables and surrounded by the pudding either sliced thinly or crumbled. The broth is served separately as a soup before the main course or alongside it to moisten the meat and pudding.

Because they could not make bread satisfactorily, the Bretons used their buckwheat flour to make galettes, or pancakes which were eaten to add bulk to eggs or vegetables or a bit of meat or fish. You will find pancakes throughout Brittany, although galettes originated in Haute-Bretagne and thinner crêpes were made in Basse-Bretagne. Today crêpes tend to be made with wheat flour and served as sweet dishes, whereas galettes continue to be made with buckwheat and usually have savoury fillings. But distinctions have become blurred and other combinations may be found.

Galettes are large, often up to twelve inches in diameter, and thin. They are cooked on a griddle called a pillig, but can be made in a frying pan if necessary. The pancake is rolled up or folded into a triangular or rectangular shape to hold a filling which may be ham or sausage or cheese, tiny shrimps or mussels, or maybe just butter or jam or honey or a fruit purée. It seems that everything on the Breton menu can turn up in a galette or crêpe, and if the filling is sweet it is likely to come with lashings of cream. The most popular drink with pancakes is buttermilk, but most crêperies have cider and beer as well.

Very thin rolled crêpes-dentelles (lace pancakes) were perfected by a baker in Quimper in 1886 and are made there commercially. Look out for them because they make an excellent accompaniment to cream and fruit desserts.

Galettes bretonnes from Pont-Aven, Fouesnant and Playben are also made commercially and well worth trying for their delicious slightly salty, buttery taste. (Make sure they are labelled pur beurre to get the real thing.)

The pig is still central to husbandry in the Argoat though he has now been joined by cows reared for their milk and to produce veal. Much pork is still cured and salted and many traditional pork and vegetable dishes survive.

Dol, the attractive cathedral town inland from St-Malo is noted for its porché, a stew made from pigs' trotters, ears, rind and bones, cooked with sorrel. It used to be left overnight in the baker's oven. Chotenn bigouden is pig's head larded with garlic and braised. Another dish from the Bigouden region is kik sal, a piece of belly pork that is rolled and roasted in the oven. Bacon ribs are roasted too and served with sliced potatoes and fried onions in a dish called arbalèze. Many of these dishes may be hard for a visitor to find because they are part of home cooking, but some country inns may serve them occasionally. You are more likely to find lard recet, a well-seasoned mixture of salt pork fat and shallots, or a dish of vegetables and pork — perhaps a bean-purée with sausages or salt pork, or a ragoût bigouden of cabbage, potatoes and onions simmered together with sausages and a piece of boiling bacon.

Not surprisingly, charcuterie is important in inland Brittany. The industry has grown in recent years to rival Alsace's position as France's chief supplier of cooked meats. The range is enormous — chitterling sausages, black and white puddings, faggots, pâtés of tripe, hare or pork, bacon and hams are particularly good. Many products are associated with a particular town. Morlaix has a reputation for its hams which are often partly cured with eau-de-vie de cidre; the white puddings (boudins blancs) of Brest may be made with cream; those of Rennes will include some chicken and will probably be served with apples, while in Dinard they still follow an old recipe for boudin aux pruneaux (prunes). Andouilles, large slicing sausages made from chitterlings, are delicious if grilled over charcoal or gently fried; the best ones come from Guémené-sur-Scorff and Ancenis. In addition to the large andouilles de Bretagne, Ancenis also produces excellent black puddings and a great variety of other sausages, while Quimperlé is famous for andouillettes, the small chitterling sausages that are grilled.

Brittany is an important poultry and egg-producing region; excellent chickens, ducks and guinea fowl are reared, most notably the plump poularde de Rennes and the caneton nantais. Poultry is usually cooked quite simply in cider or white wine; Nantais duckling is braised in Muscadet with the addition of fresh green peas. Pigeons are also found inland, and on the islands you might find a curiosity — civet de cormoron, casserole of cormorant, cooked in wine with bacon and onions.

Pré-salé lamb, that grazes on the salty coastal pastures, has a delicate fine flavour and is certainly worth finding, either roasted and served with its conventional Breton accompaniment of haricot beans (gigot à la bretonne) or braised and served with local fresh vegetables.

Sea-going and fishing have been part of the Breton way of life for centuries. The fishing industry has come through bad times and now supplies France with most of its fish and shellfish. Off the coast are caught shrimps, prawns, lobster, crab, turbot, sole, skate, grey mullet and monkfish.

These days there are substantial storage beds for crustaceans all round the coast and Brittany provides about seventy per cent of the French consumption of lobsters, crabs, crayfish and prawns. In summer the catch also includes mackerel, sardines and tuna. From St-Malo and other ports on the Channel coast the fleet goes out to fish for cod and other deep sea fish in northern waters.

Apart from St-Malo, the main fishing ports are on the sheltered southern coast — Concarneau, Douarnenez, Guilvinec, Lorient and Quiberon control most of the trade. Much of the fishing is still done on a small scale, and the fishermen follow the northerly migration of fish like the tuna, sardine and mackerel. In the spring the boats leave for southern waters looking for shoals as they make their way up towards the coast of Brittany.

Oyster and mussel beds have existed in Brittany since ancient times, and nowadays clams, scallops, abalone, cockles, winkles, whelks and sea urchins, all form part of the shellfish catch. They are taken all round the coast, but St-Brieuc is the principal port for scallops and sea urchins. Both are best in winter, particularly sea urchins, for the corals are larger and the iodine taste stronger. Try them spread on garlic bread in one of the local restaurants. Clams and the smaller shellfish are caught on both the Atlantic and the Channel coasts and are in season all year.

Brittany is famous for its oysters, flat oysters that is, not the Portuguese variety, although some of those have been introduced here. The oysters start their lives in the seed beds of the Morbihan, around Auray and Locmariaquer. The work of raising oysters and the lives of the people engaged in it are described by Eleanor Clark in *The Oysters of Locmariaquer*, (Secker and Warburg, 1964). Each oyster 'has been lifted, turned, rebedded, taught to close its mouth while travelling, culled, sorted, kept a while in a rest home or "basin" between each change of domicile, raked, protected from its enemies and shifting sands, etc, for four or five years before it gets into your mouth'. The oysters end their lives being flavoured and fattened in the maturing beds in the Bélon, Etel or Morlaix rivers. In Brittany oysters are simply called 'plates', or flat oysters; further afield the names Bélon and Cancale are particularly renowned.

Once again, first-rate fresh ingredients are treated simply. Fish are poached in court-bouillon or cooked in butter, and a little cider or wine. Most shellfish are eaten raw, or cooked just briefly as in the stuffed clam or mussel dishes that are found all round the coast. Try moules à la cancalaise, essentially mussels cooked as for moules marinières, but the sauce is enriched with butter just before serving.

Perhaps the best known Breton fish dish is cotriade, originally a fishermen's stew made from their share of the catch. It always includes a variety of white fish and oily fish, such as mackerel or sardines, and some grander versions include shellfish. Potatoes are the other essential ingredients, plus some member of the onion family — onions, leeks, shallots or garlic. The broth is usually eaten separately, followed by the fish and potatoes.

One of the reasons the Breton fishing industry survived hard times earlier this century is that canning and salting plants were set up around the coast. The salt cod industry centres on St-Malo; the Atlantic coastal towns can tuna, mackerel and sardines during the summer fishing season.

The first sardine cannery was opened in Nantes in 1824 and since that time high-quality canned sardines have been a major export from Nantes and from the nearby ports of Concarneau, Quiberon and Douarnenez. The sardines are cleaned, put briefly into a mild brine, rinsed and dried quickly in warm air, then fried lightly before being packed in cans and covered with fresh olive oil. Most cans have date marks, so look for 'vintage' sardines — many canners keep their sardines for a year or more before releasing them for sale, and they should improve for five or six years in the tin.

Brittany is blessed too with a variety of freshwater fish. There are dozens of trout streams, fishing canals, ponds and reservoirs inland. Salmon, pike, carp and eels are all common. A speciality is tiny eels called civelles, which are caught in the spring and deep-fried. The large eels are grilled or sautéed or served in cream. Pike is traditionally served with beurre blanc (see recipe p. 145), a speciality of Nantes, or it is pounded to a paste with eggs and cream and formed into quenelles which are poached. Frogs are popular too, often served with a rich cream sauce.

With its varied soils and mild climate, influenced by the Gulf Stream, Brittany grows a huge amount of vegetables and fruits. The seaweed fertiliser, used for hundreds of years all around the coast, sometimes gives vegetables the tang of the sea. The northern coast around Roscoff is famous for its cauliflowers, artichokes and new potatoes. Leeks, onions, shallots and garlic are long-established crops and market gardening areas around the towns supply tomatoes, salad greens and carrots. Rennes is another centre for artichokes, and also for asparagus and early vegetables.

For a long time the southern coast has specialised in growing vegetables for drying and for canning, originally in collaboration with the canneries started for fish. Nowadays freezing is important too. The main vegetable crops here are peas, green beans, sprouts, spinach, broad beans and haricot beans.

Plougastel is known for its strawberries, Rennes grows delicate pink-fleshed melons and there are orchards of pears and dessert apples among all the cider apple trees.

Many Breton fruits and vegetables — and fish and poultry too — are found in shops in Britain, thanks to Brittany Ferries, started in 1973 by an enterprising farmers' cooperative looking to expand its market. The regular services from Roscoff to Plymouth have improved tourist communications with Brittany too.

Bretons like hearty soups and stews with lots of vegetables. Cornouaille in the south-west has an excellent soup made with buckwheat and bacon. Beans, pumpkin, potatoes, carrots, all the onion tribe — and in fact almost every vegetable grown here — are put into some kind of stew.

Although there is a substantial dairy industry in Brittany, there is very little cheese. Most of the milk is made into cream, or into the delicious salty butter which the Bretons seem to eat with everything. The fresh cheeses, sold in small baskets in which they drain, are probably the best. Look for Crémet Nantais, or near Rennes, for Mingaux. Both have a mild creamy flavour, and may be eaten on their own at the end of a meal or with fresh fruit. St-Gildas-des-Bois is a triple cream cheese with a velvety texture and a bloomy white rind. The other local cheeses are mostly factory-made, washed-rind cheeses. St-Paulin and Campanéac are the mildest; la Meilleraye de Bretagne, made by Trappist monks, is a large, tangy cheese; Fromage du Curé, also called Nantais because it was invented by a curé from Nantes in the last century, has a strong bouquet and taste.

There may not be much Breton cheese to choose from but there are many excellent pastries and cakes made with the local butter. St-Brieuc on the Channel coast claims brioches as its own invention, although it is a claim hotly disputed by people elsewhere in France. But St-Brieuc certainly does produce wonderful, buttery brioches. So does Morlaix. Nantes has cornes — long, loaf-shaped brioches — flat cakes and biscuits. In Brittany, biscuits are synonymous with Nantes, where several biscuit manufacturers have been established since the nineteenth century.

Lorient and Quimper are famed for their cakes, and bigoudens, small cakes flavoured with almonds and eau-de-vie, are well worth trying. So is gâteau breton, a rich yeast cake with dried fruits, angelica, citrus peel or even sliced apple, that is usually served with coffee or at tea time. Kuign-aman, meaning cake and butter, is the most unusual cake. It is a yeast dough, enriched with lots of butter, and made by folding and rolling the dough to incorporate the butter, rather in the way puff pastry is made. A sweet version of far has evolved from the original grain pudding to be a type of baked custard, in some places served plain, elsewhere containing dried apricots, or prunes, or in summer, fresh cherries. Paris-Brest, a choux pastry ring filled with almonds and cream, will be found on some menus. It is thought that it was invented by Bretons living in Paris in the last century, but no one quite knows.

If you are inspecting the bakers' windows, perhaps to buy bread for a picnic, try the rye bread, or the pain d'antan (bread of yesteryear) made with mixed rye and wheat flour. Look for the excellent oat bread made with cream (pain d'avoine à la crème) — it is to be found in several towns, but that of Quimperlé is reckoned to be the best.

Drink

Cider is the usual drink in Brittany, and Fouesnant, St-Féréou and Clohars make particularly fine ciders. Lambig is an eau-de-vie made from cider. It is less refined than Normandy's calvados, but is used to good effect in cooking. You may also come across chouchen, a kind of mead made by fermenting honey.

Wine is made in Loire-Atlantique, an excellent dry white wine, Muscadet, that is best drunk young. There are three appellations for Muscadet: plain Muscadet, Muscadet de Sèvre et Maine and Muscadet Coteaux de la Loire. Quality can vary greatly, these days there are single estate Muscadets on the market alongside the cooperative wines.

Muscadet is the perfect accompaniment to fish and shellfish. Try it with a platter of fruits de mer, or a plate of oysters, or stuffed clams, or pike with beurre blanc to appreciate Breton gastronomy at its best.

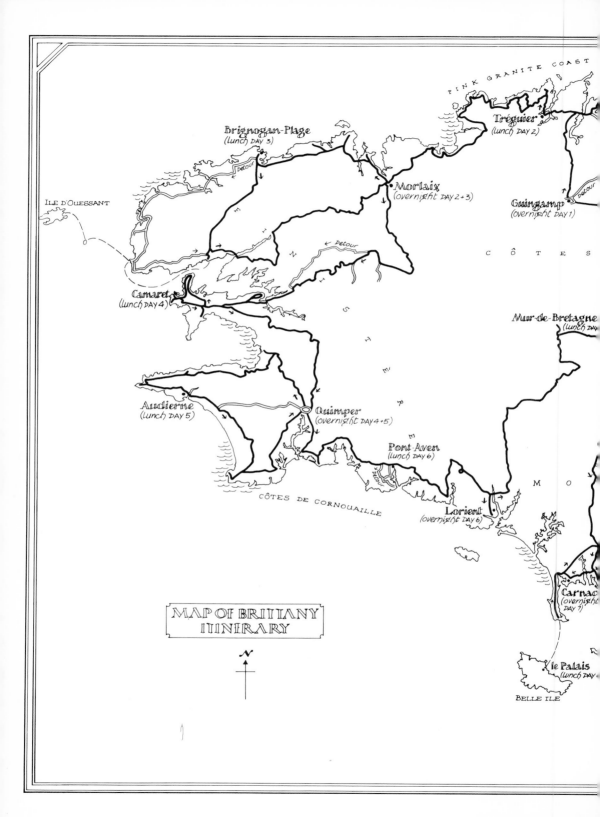

ILE D'OUESSANT

PINK GRANITE COAST

Tréguier
(lunch DAY 2)

Brignogan-Plage
(lunch DAY 3)

DETOUR

Morlaix
(overnight DAY 2 + 3)

Guingamp
(overnight DAY 1)

DETOUR

DETOUR

CÔTES

Camaret
(lunch DAY 4)

Mur-de-Bretagne
(lunch DAY)

Audierne
(lunch DAY 5)

Quimper
(overnight DAY 4 + 5)

Pont-Aven
(lunch DAY 6)

MO

CÔTES DE CORNOUAILLE

Lorient
(overnight DAY 6)

Carnac
(overnight DAY 7)

MAP OF BRITTANY
ITINERARY

N

le Palais
(lunch DAY)

BELLE ILE

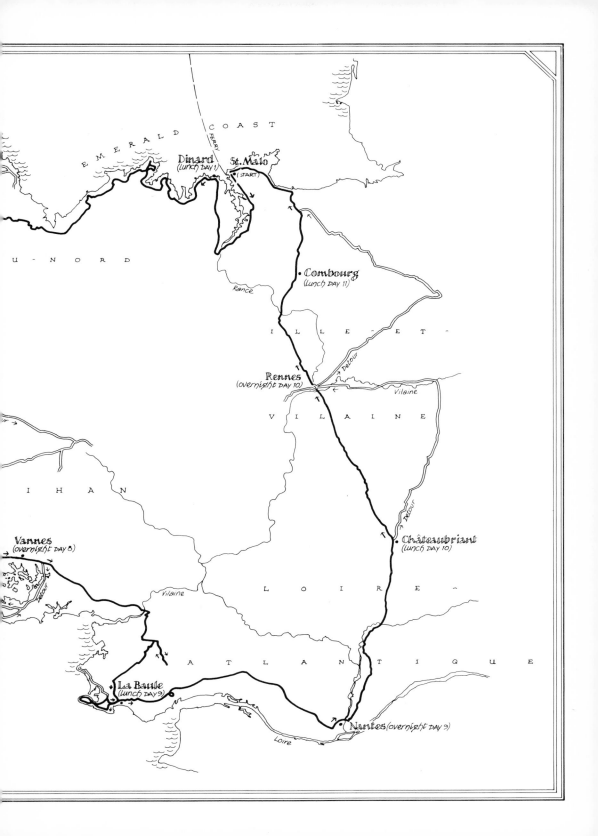

Handy Tips

HOW TO GET THERE FROM THE UK

The Itinerary begins at St-Malo. Brittany is well-served by the channel ports and car ferry companies. Most directly there is the Portsmouth-St-Malo line (9 hours), there is also the Plymouth-Roscoff link.

Cheaper, shorter crossings: Ramsgate-Dunkirk, Dover-Calais/Boulogne, Portsmouth-Le Havre, etc., can all be used with only a short drive into Brittany on arrival. However, all channel crossings tend to become heavily booked, therefore we heartily recommend making an early reservation.

WHEN TO GO

Any time from Easter to the end of September. In a good Autumn, warm sunny weather will last to the end of October.

Try to avoid travelling on or just before or after a bank holiday (see below). The worst time for traffic is the first weekend in August, when nearly every French family is on the move.

HOTELS

It is advisable to book hotels in advance especially between July and September.

CAMPING AND CARAVANNING

There are some wonderful sites throughout Brittany. Buy the green Michelin Camping and Caravanning guide for addresses. Unlike dreary England even the smallest of sites has electricity. N.B. Don't forget your Caravan Club of Great Britain registration carnet.

DRIVING

Driving on the right is usually no problem, the danger only comes when returning to the road from a car park, a petrol station and of course at roundabouts. Until recently priority was always given to those approaching from the right. This custom is fast changing and roundabouts can therefore be treated in the English style, but beware drivers turning from small roads in towns and country lanes. Traffic police can be tough even on foreign motorists who are caught speeding, overshooting a red light or failing to wear seat belts, so take care. Seat belts are obligatory everywhere in France outside town limits.

ROAD NUMBERS

The French government, which used to be responsible for numbering all the roads in France, has started to hand over the responsibility to the individual départements. In their wisdom the individual départements have in some cases decided to renumber the roads and as you can imagine this process is not only slow but confusing. I have tried to be as correct as possible with the road numbers, but you may unfortunately find some discrepancies. For example you could come across a road marked as the N137 when it is really the D937.

SPEED LIMITS

Autoroutes	130 kmph (80 mph)
Other Roads	90 kmph (56 mph)
Dual Carriageways	110 kmph (68 mph)
Built-up areas or as directed by signs	60 kmph (37 mph)

Autoroutes nearly all have periodic tolls (péages) and can be expensive on long journeys.

THE METRIC SYSTEM

Kilometres — for road distances 8 km equals 5 miles thus:

Km:miles	Km:miles	Km:miles	Km:miles
3:2	8:5	40:25	90:56
4:2½	9:5½	50:31	100:62
5:3	10:6	60:37	125:78
6:3½	20:12	70:44	150:94
7:4	30:18	80:50	200:125

BANK HOLIDAYS

New Year's Day	1st January
Easter Monday	Variable
Labour Day	1st May
V.E. Day	8th May
Ascension Day	6th Thursday after Easter
Whit Monday	2nd Monday after Ascension
Bastille Day	14th July
Assumption	15th August
All Saints (Toussaint)	1st November
Armistice Day	11th November
Christmas Day	25th December

BANKS

Banks are shut on Saturdays and Sundays, except in towns with a Saturday market, when they open on Saturday and shut on Monday. Banks also close at midday on the eve of bank holidays. Banking hours are normally 8 a.m.–12 noon and 2–4.30 p.m. When changing cheques or travellers' cheques remember your passport and Eurocheque encashment card or other internationally recognised cheque card.

SHOP OPENING TIMES

These vary according to a) season b) type of shop c) size of town. In most places shops are open on Saturday, but may be shut on Monday. Food shops (baker, butcher, general store) tend to shut later than others, sometimes as late as 7 p.m., some open on Sundays and bank holiday mornings. Generally all shops close for 2–3 hours at lunchtime from midday.

RAILWAYS

S.N.C.F. — Société Nationale de Chemin de Fer. The trains are generally very clean, comfortable and punctual. It is best to buy tickets in advance from mainline stations or travel agents. Seats can be reserved on main lines. Hire cars can be booked in advance in most large towns. Bicycles can be hired at stations. Men over 65 and women over 60, on production of their passport, can obtain a 'carte vermeil' entitling them to a 50% reduction on non-rush hour trains.

Note: Many stations have automatic punch ticket machines (red machine) on the platform, this dates your ticket. If you do not get your ticket punched by one of these machines you can be charged again, plus a fine of 20% so be careful.

MONUMENTS AND MUSEUMS

Opening times and prices of admission have not been included in this book, as they are subject to change. All places mentioned are open to the public and will charge a few francs admission. Normally they will be open from Easter to the end of October, from 9.30–12.00 a.m. and from 3–5 p.m.

Note: Guided tours will cease admission half an hour before closing. Check with the local tourist office for details.

KEY TO ITINERARY
Ratings are for prices/room/night.

| ★★ | Reasonable | ★★★★ | Expensive |
| ★★★ | Average | ★★★★★ | Very expensive |

Names of the hotels and restaurants are printed in bold and are distinguished by the following symbols:

Lunch   Dinner

The itinerary provides a basic route for each day and, for those with time available, offers suggestions for additional trips marked in the text as Detours.

Text Maps.
The map on p. 30-1 shows the complete itinerary.

The Itinerary

PINK GRANITE COAST

ILE DE BRÉ

Ploumanach
Trégastel-Plage
ILE GRANDE
Perros-Guirec
Trébeurden

Plougrescant
Port-Blanc
Trestel
St Gonery

POINTE DE L'ARCOUEST

Paimpol

D786

Tréguier
(lunch
DAY 2)

Lannion

D786

Locquirec

St Michel-en-Grève

D786

Lanmeur

St Efflam

D786

N12

Morlaix (overnight DAY 2)

D787

→ Detour Day 2

D9

Guingamp (overnight

N12

DAY 1·2

N

POINT DU
GROUIN

Cancale

CAP FRÉHEL

Fort de la Latte

la Motte

St Cast

St.Lunaire   Dinard   St.Malo

St Quay-Portrieux

Étables-sur-Mer

Binic

Erquy

Sables
d'Or-
les-Pins

St Jacut-
de-la-Mer

St Briac

Lancieux

le Val-André

(lunch) DAY 1

D786

D54

D13

D786

N137

D768

D786

D786

D412

Dinan

rieux

St-Malo

DAY 1

St-Malo to Guingamp: approx 110 miles.

The holiday begins at St-Malo, gateway to Brittany. There is much to see behind the ramparts of the old town before following the Rance river south to Dinan, one of the best-preserved, walled, medieval cities in Brittany. Dinard, Queen of the Coast, proves an ideal place for lunch, before spending the afternoon sampling the beauty of the Emerald Coast westwards to St-Brieuc. A short drive across country leads to Guingamp for dinner.

Travels in Brittany

Arrive at St-Malo

St-Malo

Most English visitors to Brittany come to St-Malo, the province's sea gateway. I shall always remember the time I arrived there in the early hours of the morning. The old walled city of the corsairs on the small rocky peninsula seemed to slowly slide out of a mist, like a spectre, a mirage, its pinkish granite towers and turrets peering above tall walls. It resembled a ghost, which in a sense it was, as old St-Malo had been destroyed back in 1944 during a two-week siege, when it was pounded to death by the Americans. The Germans clung to this treasure for as long as they could, leaving only its ruin.

However, the old walled town, 'Intra Muros', has been most painstakingly restored, and you can still walk round the magnificent ramparts, built to withstand the hammering of mighty waves — their great strength even enabled them to withstand the war's battering — and imagine you are back in medieval times.

Enter by St-Vincent's gateway and take the staircase to the right for a walk around the old town. From many points there are magnificent views of the coast. An aquarium has been built into the walls of the ramparts in Place Vauban, near St-Thomas Gate, while the Quic-en-Groigne tower of the castle in Chateaubriand Place contains a waxworks museum, displaying the historic events of St-Malo. Inside the castle the Historic Museum in the Grand Donjan records the city's development and gives information and mementoes of its celebrities, such as Chateaubriand, Lamannais (Catholic radical), Jacques Cartier (who discovered the mouth of the St. Lawrence river), Duguay-Trouin and Surcouf (two of St-Malo's best-known privateers). St-Vincent's cathedral, a dignified and spacious blending of old Gothic with modern style, has been most carefully reconstructed. Jacques Cartier has a simple tomb, and a stone marks the spot where he stood in May, 1535, to receive the benediction of the Bishop of St-Malo before his next departure to the New World. Note the new stained-glass windows by Max Ingrand (1908–1969).

Just offshore lies the islet of Le Grand Bé (it can be visited at low tide), where stands the tomb of Chateaubriand. He wished to be buried on this lonely rock, surrounded by the sea which had first inspired him.

St-Malo was named after Maclou or Malo, a 6th-century priest from Wales, who converted the inhabitants of a nearby town (now St-Servan) to Christianity and became their first Bishop. The island was uninhabited until the 8th century when the surrounding people sought refuge on the rock from the Normans. The bishopric was moved there in 1444. Under the control of the Bishops, St-Malo developed along its own independent lines. During the Wars of Religion, it even managed to establish a Republic which lasted four years. During the 17th century it became the headquarters of the French East India Company. Many of its inhabitants reaped large fortunes from piracy in the English channel. Although bombarded in retaliation by the English in 1693, 1695 and 1758, the town was not finally finished as a Corsair centre until 1856.

St-Malo (old town and new inland one), St-Servan, Paramé (saltwater spa) and Rothéneuf have now joined up into one large town resort. St-Servan on St-Malo's rocky side faces the Rance river. Grande Plage, a long stretch of sand, with a promenade behind, runs between the old walled town and Paramé, interrupted by a rocky promontory which joins St-Malo beach and Casino beach with Rochebonne beach. Rothéneuf, further west, also has two good beaches; Val is small and attractive, the other, Plage-du-Havre, is large but almost landlocked (like an inland lake, and so popular for water sports) by dunes and rocky cliffs.

St-Malo is a good place for excursions, both by land — Mont-St-Michel, and along the Emerald Coast — and by sea to the Channel Islands, the Chausey Isles and Cézembre Isle (zoological reserve). We shall take the route to Dinan via the Rance and then on to the coastal resorts.

Eastwards from St-Malo lies Pointe du Grouin, a wild rocky headland, from which there is a good view of the coast from Mont-St-Michel to Cap Fréhel. South of the Pointe lies Cancale, a picturesque and important fishing port. The port's fame is mainly due to its oyster beds — gourmets come from far and wide to sample their fruits. Cancale was the birthplace of Jeanne Jugan (1792–1879), foundress of a religious order called 'Little Sisters of the Poor'. Jeanne's father, a fisherman, was drowned at sea leaving a widow and seven children. Jeanne became a domestic servant with an old lady and also helped look after old, poor and lonely people. With a small inheritance left her by the old lady she bought a humble home where the people she helped could find shelter. Later with the help of other poor women, she founded a religious society which in time grew to become the Congregation of the Little Sisters of the Poor. Today there are 6,500 sisters in 300 establishments scattered all over the world.

Take the N137, then D29 and N176 from St-Malo south, travelling alongside or near the Rance for most of the way, to Dinan.

Dinan

In spite of the number of tourists and shoppers Dinan is one of the best-preserved, walled, medieval towns in Brittany, and is still a pleasure to wander around. Beautifully situated above the head of the Rance Estuary, it is an important and busy road centre for the province's north-east region.

Start your tour from Jardin Anglais, built in terraces on the site of St-Sauveur's cemetery, and the Promenade de la Duchesse Anne along the old ramparts to the Promenade des Petits Fosses. The castle, an enormous oval-shaped tower, was built by the Duke of Brittany in the 14th century. It has five storeys, a spiral stone staircase, and contains a museum of local history.

In the Place du Guesclin, you will see an equestrian statue of this celebrated Breton commander, a reminder of the 14th-century single combat that took place here between him and Canterbury, an English knight who had captured his brother, Olivier, while Dinan was being besieged by the Duke of Lancaster. Needless to say, du Guesclin won. His brother was released and received the 1000 florins' ransom demanded.

Dinan has often been called du Guesclin's town, and indeed, he married a Dinan girl, and asked that he be buried here. His wishes were only partially carried out, as his body had to be brought some distance across France, and bits of it got left behind on the way. In the end, perhaps appropriately, the town only received his heart, which now resides in St-Sauveur's church.

Dinard

Follow the D766 to Dinard which faces St-Malo across the Rance estuary. It can also be approached direct from St-Malo either by ferry boat, or by road across the Rance dam. This dam, completed in 1967, was the first sea-powered generating station in the world. Its turbines use the exceptionally high rise and fall of the tides to produce electricity (some 550 million Kws a year). It may be visited. An illuminated diagram and dioramas are displayed in a gallery. The machinery may be seen from a balcony.

Dinard is somewhat staid but smart, and could well be called the Bournemouth of Brittany. It is certainly the 'Queen' of this part of the coast. Up to about the middle of the last century, it was a mere hamlet and fishing village, an appendage to St-Enogat. Then it was discovered by a rich American, Mr Coppinger, who fell in love with the place and decided to stay. His example was followed by others, especially the English, who built themselves houses along the coast. Although other nationalities come here too, it still retains a sort of superior-English-seaside-resort flavour.

Dinard boasts an aquarium, casino and a magnificent dance hall. There are parks, an indoor heated swimming-pool, and exceptionally fine sandy beaches, ideal for children. The climate is good, and you can walk in peace along the pedestrianised Promenade Clair de Lune to Pointe du Moulinet, from which there are magnificent views of the coast. Golf and tennis tournaments, regattas and an international horse show draw vast crowds here during the summer. Dinard is also good for excursions by road, rail or boat.

Lunch at Le Grand Hôtel, Dinard.

The Emerald Coast

This stretch of coast, broken, picturesque and rocky, lies between the Grouin point and Le Val-André, and is shared between departments Ille-et-Vilaine and Côtes-du-Nord. Although the road does not always skirt the coast, it is one of continual interest, but becomes very crowded in summer.

Many fashionable and family resorts are situated along this coastline. Continue westwards from Dinard (D786) past St-Lunaire, smartish with two good beaches, to St-Briac, a pretty little resort with plenty of sandy beaches and picturesque harbour. It also has one of the best golf-courses in France, which it shares with Dinard. Lancieux is quiet in unspoiled surroundings and has long stretches of beaches. St-Jacut-de-la-Mer is a small fishing port, village and seaside resort. Le Guildo is pictuesquely sited on the shore of Arguenon estuary, not far from a ruined castle, once the 15th-century seat of Gilles de

Bretagne, a happy-go-lucky and gallant poet, who was murdered by his brother, the reigning duke.

Continuing along the coast St-Cast is another favourite resort, but made up of four parts: Les Mielles (mostly hotels and important villas), L'Isle (a rocky corner bordering a long beach on its northern side), Bourg (the main town) and La Garde (resembling a wooded park).

Unfortunately, the road does not follow all the coastal indentations; even so there are many fine views. From the Pointe de St-Cast, as from many other rocky outcrops, these are quite splendid. Most impressive of all is that of Cap Fréhel (D16), its 200ft pink, grey and black granite cliffs stand sheer above the sea, fringed by rocks on which waves pound furiously. Popular both with tourists and nesting birds, it is one of the most grandiose sights on the Breton coast, especially in the evenings. Near the village of La Motte is the medieval (but restored in the 17th century) Fort de la Latte (built by the Guyon-Matignons as a fortress to protect St-Malo; Vauban, France's great military engineer, later added to its fortifications), superbly sited on rugged cliffs. It can be reached over the drawbridge. Guided tours are available. After Cap Fréhel, the coast descends less savagely via Sables d'Or-les-Pins (D34), a spacious modern but somewhat characterless resort with hotels set amid pinewoods and dunes to Erquy (D786) a small but growing, pleasantly busy fishing-port renowned for its scallops. Finally, Le Val-André, the last resort on the Emerald Coast, is a rather staid although popular family resort: it boasts one of the best beaches on this coast.

Bay of St-Brieuc

The bay of St-Brieuc sweeps down in a rough curve from Pointe de l'Arcouest in the west to Sables d'Or-les-Pins. In the centre, St-Brieuc, a large busy town, is the business and commercial heart of the Côtes-du-Nord. Situated about 5 miles from the sea on a plateau, divided by the Gouëdic and Gouet rivers, there is not very much of interest to see here, except its cathedral. St-Étienne (13th- to 14th-century) is a church fortress: thus it combines two massive towers complete with arrow-slit windows, supported by buttresses, with the more usual religious decor, such as 15th-century stained-glass windows. To see old houses walk through the Place du Martray and Rue Fardel. The Hôtel des Ducs de Bretagne once sheltered James II after he was deposed from the English throne in 1688. St-Brieuc got its name from the Welsh monk, Brieuc, who is supposed to have lived here in the 5th century. His fountain is to be seen in the chapel Notre-Dame-de-la-Fontaine. There are some appetizing food markets at St-Brieuc. Saturday is the best day.

Follow the D412/N12 from St-Brieuc to Guingamp.

Dinner and overnight at Hôtel Hermine, Guincamp.

Le Grand Hôtel
46 Avenue George V
35801 Dinard
Tel: 99 46 10 28

Start off in style with lunch at this hotel redolent of Dinard's elegant heyday. The bar and terrace overlook the sea.

Closed:	November to March
Rooms:	100
Facilities:	Bar, restaurant, terrace, garden, car park
Credit cards:	Visa, Eurocard, American Express
Food:	Smart with mid-meal sorbets. Seafood and fish a speciality.
Rating:	★★★★

USEFUL INFORMATION: DINARD

Tourist Office:	2 Boulevard Feart
	Tel: 99 46 94 12
Population:	10,016
Amenities:	Casino, golf course, small airfield

USEFUL INFORMATION: ST-MALO

Tourist Office:	Esplanade St Vincent
	Tel: 99 56 64 48
Population:	47,329
Amenities:	Casino, passenger ferry, small airport

USEFUL INFORMATION: ST BRIEUC

Tourist Office:	Rue St Gouéno
	Tel: 96 33 32 50
Population:	51,399
Amenities:	Golf

Bar Hôtel L'Hermine
1 Boulevard Clemenceau
22200 Guingamp
Tel: 96 21 02 56

A good value, friendly establishment.

Open all year	
Rooms:	12
Facilities:	Bar, restaurant grill
Credit cards:	Visa
Food:	Extremely reasonable, they offer three variations on Coquilles St Jacques
Rating:	★★

USEFUL INFORMATION: GUINGAMP

Tourist Office:	2 Place du Vally
	Tel: 96 43 73 89
Population:	9,519

DAY 2

Guingamp to Morlaix: approx. 100 miles.

After rambling through the old quarter of Guingamp, head directly
northwards to Paimpol, the Pointe de l'Arcouest and the picturesque scenery
of the Pink Granite Coast. Alternatively you could detour along the western
edge of St-Brieuc Bay, and include a visit to the unique Île de Bréhat before
reaching Paimpol.

Lunch at Tréguier is followed by a drive along the coast to Locquirec, where
the legendary land of Finistère begins. And so to Morlaix, one of the old pirate
capitals of Finistère, and the next overnight stop.

Morlaix

Breakfast at Guingamp.

Guingamp

Although Guingamp's château has been demolished, the old quarter's narrow winding streets have not lost their charm. A fountain, La Plomée, surmounted by the Virgin surrounded by a variety of carved stone animals, tumbles down over three basins in the main square. Behind stands Notre-Dame-de-Bon-Secours (12th- to 15th-century). To see inside is the Black Virgin, the town's patroness who plays an important part in the church's Great Pardon. The 13th-century clock tower (L) and Renaissance tower (R) stand either side of a fine delicately-decorated doorway. Rather incongruously, the church is Gothic on the left and Renaissance on the right.

Guingamp stands on the River Trieux. Follow the D787 north along the winding river valley and then head towards Paimpol.

Detour

Alternatively, you can take the D9 to the coast and travel up St-Brieuc Bay (D786) to Paimpol.

There are plenty more sandy beaches on the west side of the bay, but the resorts are less interesting. Three are Binic, a pretty yachting and fishing port, Étables-sur-Mer, which has two sheltered beaches and a fine public park and St-Quay-Portrieux, popular, with four sandy beaches. It is made up of two towns — Portrieux (south), a small fishing port and St-Quay, a resort with casino. You can get a boat from here to the colourful Île de Bréhat, whose pinky-grey rocks contrast with the blue-grey sea. About 2 miles long and a mile wide, it is really two strips of land joined by a narrow tongue. Little paths run through it. Because it has a mild climate and little rain, many exotic plants, such as fig trees, myrtle, oleander and mimosa, flourish here. Cars are not allowed but you can ride on a tractor! Fishermen are supposed to have sailed to the New World from here before it was discovered by Christopher Columbus.

Paimpol

Paimpol, a busy port and market town, has some charming narrow cobbled streets, old houses and squares, behind the harbour. Pierre Loti, author of

Pecheur d'Islande (Fishermen of Iceland, 1866) helped to popularise Paimpol. The 16th-century houses in Place du Montray, where he stayed, he made the home of Gaud, his heroine. Paimpol harbour, once renowned as a deep-sea cod fishing port is now used for inland fishing and sailing boats. Oyster cultivation and early vegetable markets are two important sources of revenue.

From Pointe de l'Arcouest (D789), about 3½ miles to the north of Paimpol, is a good view of the bay, especially at high tide. From here you can also take a boat to the Isle of Bréhat (see above).

The Pink Granite Coast

This stretch of coast lies roughly between L'Arcouest and the bay of Lannion; it is renowned for its rose-coloured cliffs which can be seen from far out at sea. Behind lies a lush green region blessed with a mild climate.

The drive between Paimpol and Tréguier crosses two bridges over the estuaries and affords some grandiose views.

Tréguier

Tréguier, a town of character, is built in terraces up a hill, overlooking the estuary formed by the junction of the Jaudy and Guindy rivers. Its 13th- to 15th-century cathedral is one of the finest in Brittany and, with its cloister, forms a most delightful ensemble in the central square, Place du Martroy.

Tréguier is particularly celebrated for its Pardon, held annually on 19th May, in honour of St Yves (1253–1303), advocate of the poor, who was born at nearby Minihy Tréguier, where a church now stands. He is one of Brittany's most popular saints, and the patron of the legal profession. Ernest Renan (1823–1892), historian and philosopher, a rather different sort of thinker — his faith was science — was born in Tréguier too. The house in which he was born and lived has been turned into a museum.

Lunch at Le Kastell Dinec'h, Tréguier.

From Tréguier you can take the D8 up to Plougrescant (where massive rocks seem about to squash the house set between them). At the church of St-Gonery were discovered impressive 16th-century paintings.

Continue westwards to Port-Blanc (D31/74). This is another attractive unspoilt little fishing port, with large rocks and boulders surrounding its bay. Its 16th-century stone chapel blends picturesquely into the scene. The beach here is not very good -- holidaymakers will have to go further afield to Trestel.

Perros-Guirec

Follow the indentations of the coast to Perros-Guirec, two villages joined together which have become one of Brittany's largest resorts. The first part of its name is derived from Pen-Roz, the last from St Guirec, an early priest. Now popular and quite fashionable, it boasts a casino, two beaches and some very pleasant walks. It has an interesting church, squat Romanesque (12th- and 14th-century) built out of pink granite, and a chapel, Notre-Dame-de-la-Clarté, built by a Breton noble who, when lost at sea, vowed he would build a chapel on whatever part of the coast emerged first out of the fog to give him his bearings.

The best part of Perros-Guirec, in my view, is the winding rocky walk, the Sentier des Douaniers, starting from Plage de Tresraou and along the coast, between Perros-Guirec, and Ploumanach, a delightful small fishing-port resort. You can take a boat from Perros-Guirec around the fascinating bird sanctuaries (include gannets, guillemots, penguins, great black-backed gulls, puffins, crested cormorants and oyster-catchers and petrels), on the Sept Îles. You can land on the Île des Moines for an hour and visit the old gunpowder factory, lighthouse, ruined Vauban fort and former monastery with tiny chapel.

From Perros-Guirec begins the *Corniche Bretonne* (D788) and one of the best parts of the pink granite coast. Here granite rocks have been chipped and chiselled by the elements, predominantly the sea, into a variety of strange shapes, which have been given names by the locals. See if you can spot the 'witch', the 'rabbit', the 'umbrella', the 'corkscrew', even 'Napoleon's hat'.

Trégastel-Plage, a small scattered resort, has its share of interestingly-shaped rocks. There is the pile known as the 'tortues' (tortoises), and on the Grève

Blanche you can see the 'tire bouchon' (corkscrew) and the great rock known as 'Roi Gradlon'. Trégastel Bourg, just inland from Trégastel-Plage, has a 12th- to 13th-century church and calvary, standing on a hill. There are many islands off this part of the coast, the largest of which is Île Grande, which is connected to the mainland by a road.

Trébeurden, a family resort and small port, has several beaches. The main two are separated by a rocky peninsula, on which stands a rocky mound, Le Castel, from which there are good views over the coast.

Inland from Trébeurden (D65), lies Lannion, a port and commercial centre on the Léguer (salmon-fishing) river, linking the coast with Tréguier and Guingamp — a good place for reaching this coast's famous beaches and starting on inland excursions. Lannion possesses a very picturesque old town, but it is also a centre for communications and electronic research. Nearby is a huge white plastic dome, the grand Pleumeur Bodou space-telecommunication centre.

Follow the D786 to St-Michel-en-Grève, noted for its small sailors' church and cemetery as well as the Lannion races in the bay. The Lieue-de-Grève, a magnificent 2½ miles' long beach, skirts the base of the bay. Here the tide retreats over a mile at low tide. Steep headlands follow. The Corniche de l'Armorique lies between St-Efflam (named after an Irish saint who landed here in 740 AD) and Locquirec, a small lively fishing port, marina and resort with attractive church and wide sandy beach, it follows a very picturesque indented coast. At Locquirec you are in Finistère, the mysterious land of the west.

Finistère

This is the mystical Brittany of legend and wide skies, of rugged rocks, rough seas and sand. Here the two peninsulas of France, the Abers and La Cornouaille, end in what has been described as the open jaws of a dragon with the Crozon Peninsula wedged like a tongue between. It is a head set against and defying the crashing sea waves, the storms, the gales. Some parts are dramatic, some windswept and bleak. Inland, behind the defences, and especially in the south, are coves, beaches, inlets, lush green countryside, ideal for camping, boating and family holidays. Finistère — 'the end of the earth' — is not one complete region and has, in fact, three capitals, Morlaix in the north, Brest in the northwest and Quimper in the south. We head first for Morlaix (D64, D786).

Morlaix

Morlaix is a busy, pleasant town, climbing steep valleys around a high 200-ft, two-storeyed viaduct bridge (built 1861–64), spanning Places des Otages, its market place. Its many twisting narrow streets, particularly the picturesque Grande Rue, make it a delight to wander through. To see there especially are St-Melaine (founded in the 12th century) and St-Mathieu (demolished 1821 and rebuilt 1824) which possesses an unusual treasure, a 15th-century statue of the Virgin, which opens to reveal a figure holding Christ on the cross. Excavations of the peninsula on the east side of Morlaix estuary have uncovered a great tumulus containing important megalithic groupings.

Morlaix's early history is still being unravelled but other remains found in the vicinity suggest there was a Roman occupation of the site. Its name may be derived from Mons Relaxus. The Counts of Léon held lordships here in the 12th century, but this was disputed by the Dukes of Brittany. Morlaix was captured by the English in 1187 and 1522.

Its port on the Dassen (now known as the Morlaix river), a tidal inlet of the channel, became increasingly important over the centuries. From the 15th to the 18th century Morlaix's harbour was one of the largest and most important in Lower Brittany. The shipowners were mainly involved in piracy, which in 1552 led to a major attack on the town. As privateers from Morlaix had sacked Bristol, 60 English ships sailed into her bay in a surprise revenge attack. Most of the townspeople were away attending fairs at Guingamp and Noyal-Pontivy, thus leaving the English a free hand to ransack the town. Unfortunately, they celebrated their victory too soon: many fell asleep in a drunken stupor in Styvel woods. Here they were massacred by the returning men of Morlaix.

To guard against such attacks the people of Morlaix built Taureau castle at Carantec at the entrance to the port. Another memorial to the event was the addition of a lion facing an English leopard on the town's coat of arms and the words 'S'ils le mordent, mord les' (If they bite you, bite them).

Fortunately, today's peaceful town appears to have forgotten its bloodthirsty past. The port, no longer very important, is now used chiefly for pleasure-craft and boats carrying fruit and vegetables. Morlaix makes a good centre for exploring the Abers peninsula. At Morlaix you will find there are many very good eating places including, of course, numerous crêperies.

Dinner and overnight at Hôtel d'Europe, Morlaix.

Kastell Dinec'h
Route de Lannion
Tréguier
Tel: 96 92 49 39

Closed: 25 October to 31 December, and Tuesday evenings and
                   Wednesdays.
Credit cards: Visa, Eurocard
Rating: ★★★

USEFUL INFORMATION: TRÉGUIER

Tourist Office: à la Mairie
                   Tel: 96 92 30 19
Population: 3,400

Hôtel d'Europe
1 rue Aiguillon
29210 Morlaix
Tel: 98 62 11 99

With some fine seventeenth-century wood panelling in the reception area,
this hotel is smart and modern despite its reasonable prices.

Closed: January
Rooms: 68
Facilities: Bar, restaurant
Credit cards: American Express, Carte Bleu, Diners Club, Eurocard
Food: Local dishes, cider and apples are used a lot
Rating: ★★

Auberge des Gourmets
90 rue Gambetta
Morlaix
Tel: 98 88 06 06

A restaurant only but it serves good value good food, so worth a visit.

Closed:	Mid-October to mid-November and Mondays
Credit cards:	Visa
Rating:	★★

USEFUL INFORMATION: MORLAIX

Tourist Office:	Place Otages
	Tel: 98 62 14 94
Population:	19,541

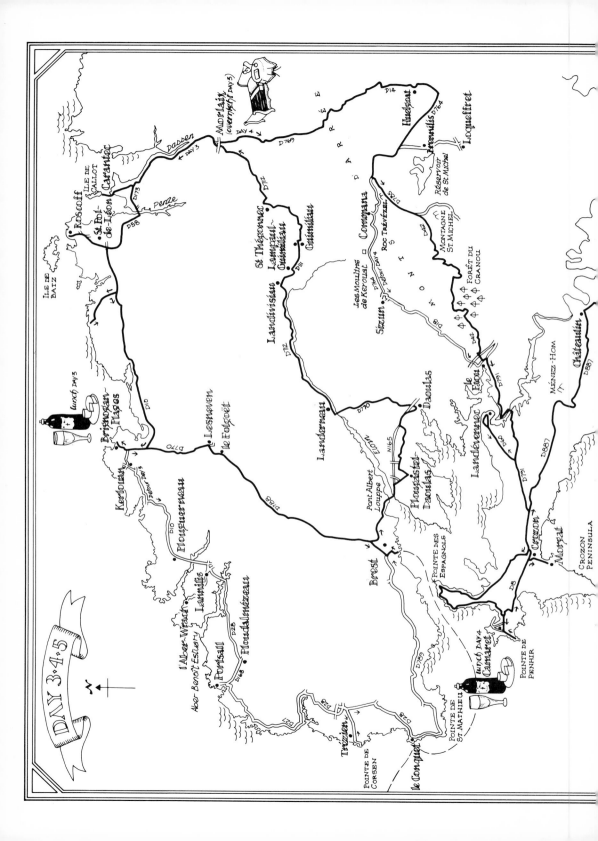

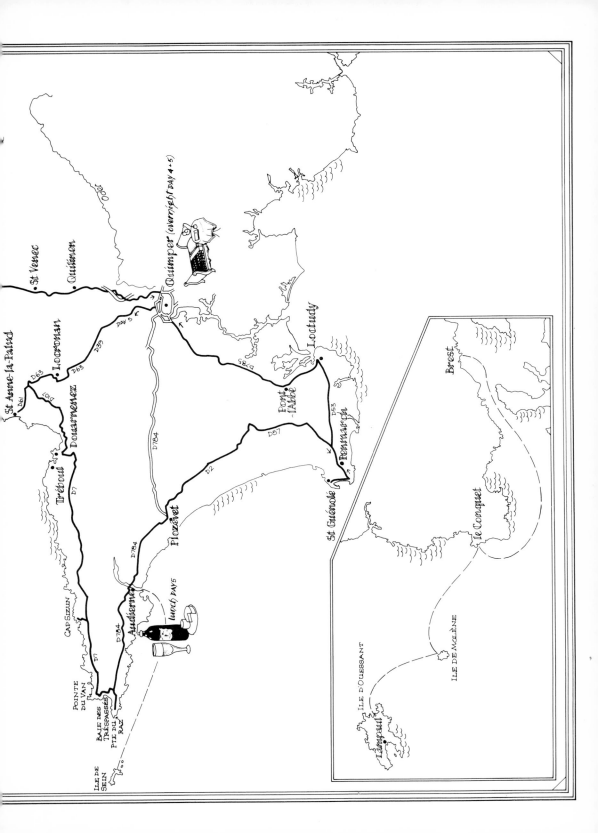

St-Thégonnec Calvary

DAY 3

Morlaix to Brest to Morlaix: approx. 110 miles.

Today's route circles the northern promontory of Finistère, the land of mists and myths, bounded by a jagged, rocky coastline. Heading northwards first towards the fashionable and family resort of Carantec and the old port of Roscoff, continue west along the coast to Brignogan-Plages for lunch.

In the afternoon you can either follow the magnificent coastal road, crossing the Abers Estuary, down to Le Conquet and east to Brest or cross the peninsula direct to Brest via the shrine of legend — Le Folgoët. From Brest we follow the Élorn inland to the rival calvaries of Guimiliau and St-Thégonnec before returning to Morlaix.

Breakfast at Morlaix.

Follow the Dassen valley (D173/73) to Carantec, which stands on the coast between the estuaries of the Penzé, and Morlaix rivers. It is a pleasant family resort with several bathing beaches and any walk you take will offer rewarding views in all directions, over the pinewoods, the estuaries and out over the islands. Nearby Callot Island can be reached on foot at low tide. The town has retained the traditional Breton architecture wherever possible. There is a pardon here on the Sunday following 15th August.

Crossing the Penzé estuary (D173/58) and turning north towards Roscoff, take time first to stop at St-Pol-de-Léon, standing on a plateau. St-Pol is a busy centre for early vegetables. Its name 'Pol' comes from Paulus 'the Aurelian', a Cumbrian monk who came here about 517 AD via the islands of Ouessant and Batz. St-Pol-de-Léon, also known as Kastel Paol, was the first Bishopric of Léon in Lower Brittany.

Because of its position near a port and surrounded by fertile land, it soon became a wealthy town. Its fine cathedral (built in the 13th, 14th, 15th and 16th centuries) well-proportioned and elegant (inspired by the cathedral at Coutances) and magnificent belfry or Kreisker chapel (14th- and 15th-century) 77 metres high (inspired by St-Pierre's spire at Caen) are landmarks in the surrounding flat countryside.

The tombs of the town's bishops are to be found in the cathedral. The last one, François de la Marche, was an emigrée, along with many other eminent Bretons during the Revolutionary period. His Bishopric, St-Pol, did not survive Napoleon.

Roscoff

The old port of Roscoff is sturdy, grey and picturesque with plenty of narrow streets and aged granite houses. It has an interesting 16th-century church, Notre-Dame Kraz-Baz, which boasts one of the finest Renaissance belfries in Finistère, while its outside walls and towers are decorated with sculptured ships and cannons, a reminder of its pirating days. The Charles Pérez aquarium, an important French marine laboratory, with a very good collection of fish and sea creatures, especially shellfish, was founded here by Professor de Lacaze Duthiers in 1872.

Roscoff, whose name was once Roc'h-Kroun, and later Rosco Coz went through hard times in its early days. It was invaded by Vikings, ravaged by the English, captured by du Guesclin. Later, like St-Malo, it became a centre for corsairs. In 1548, the five-year-old Mary Queen of Scots landed here (she was engaged to the French Dauphin) and, some 100 years later, her descendant Bonny Prince Charlie arrived here after Culloden.

Apart from its ferry harbour and lobster port, the old town of Roscoff is probably most famous for the vegetables — cauliflowers, artichokes and onions — grown in surrounding fields, in a region known as the *Ceinture Dorée*, 'the golden belt'. From Roscoff you can take a boat across to the treeless island of Batz on which stands a fishing village, a lighthouse and a garden of tropical plants. It has some good beaches. Most of the men who live there are fishermen or sailors; the women work in the fields, or collect seaweed. As with the rest of Léon's northern coast, Roscoff specialises in the collection and use of seaweed. There are over 70 varieties. Mixed with shells and sea mud it is used to improve the soil. Roscoff's beach, Plage des Bains, is small and not very good — too much seaweed appears at low tide. The nearest good one is about 12 miles away at Téven-Kerbrat Kerfissen, backed by dunes. There is another one at Pors Guen, further west still.

Now that there is a regular ferry service between Pymouth and Roscoff, Roscoff is quite a good place for a short stay, as it is within easy reach of some interesting places. But as local bus services are not very good, you would be advised to bring a car.

Brignogan-Plages

Brignogan-Plages, further west along the D10, is an attractive family resort with a small harbour and very wide sandy beaches stretching for nearly three miles. Piles of rock on either side, some curiously shaped, can make it appear bleak. There are very few trees. It was along this wild coast incidentally that the Amoca Cadiz was wrecked, spilling oil as high waves whipped by 100-mph winds smashed the ship's hull against the rock. About 300 miles of this part of Brittany's coastline was polluted.

You can hire kayaks from the Club Nautique (active here) for exploring the rugged coast, thus enabling you to see the oddly-shaped rocks in more detail. To see nearby is the Menhir of Men-Marz (Miracle) standing 8ft tall.

Lunch at Castel Régis, Brignogan-Plages.

North-West Finistère

This region, famous for its legends, is known as the Abers — estuaries (a Welsh word as well as a Breton one). Its low-lying hills, broken up by rivers and shallow streams, are often hidden mysteriously behind mists. Small islands surround the seaweed-draped coast.

Detour

To take the coastal route along the peninsula to Brest is time-consuming but rewarding. The coast here is spectacular and rugged. From Brignogan head first for Kerlouan (more strangely shaped rocks and two menhirs), then on to Plouguerneau. Take your time crossing the Aber-Wrac'h estuary (D13) to Lannilis and enjoy the view from the road. Across the bleak moorland stands Aber-Wrac'h at the head of the inlet, renowned for its oysters.

Crossing the Aber-Benoit estuary (D28/26) return to the coast by Portsall (small family resort) and follow the coast road to Pointe de Corsen, whose 160ft cliff stands on France's most westerly tip. The Trézien lighthouse (182 steps to the top) marks the division between the Channel and the Atlantic. South lies Le Conquet, a picturesque grey-granite fishing port and resort on the southern end of the promontory. At Pointe de St-Mathieu the famous lighthouse offers splendid views from the top. Take the D789 to Brest.

Le Folgoët

To the south of Brignogan just past Lesneven lies Le Folgoët (D770, D788), famous for its magnificent church of Our Lady, which possesses a particularly fine 15th-century carved granite rood-screen; its great Pardon (first Sunday in September), one of the biggest in Brittany; and its legend.

In the chapel porch there is a fountain fed by a spring under the altar. Legend has it that a fool named Salaun, nicknamed Folgoët (fool of the wood) lived by a spring in a wood. The only words he knew, and endlessly repeated, were 'O Lady Virgin Mary'. After he died a white lily was found growing in the wood. The fool's words were marked out by the pistils in the flower. When they dug up the lily they discovered it was growing out of the fool's mouth. The Duke of Montfort was at that time battling in the Wars of Succession and had vowed that he would raise a church to the Virgin if he were victorious. After winning the battle of Auray he decided his church should be built at Le Folgoët to commemorate the miracle. The altar was placed over the fool's woodland spring.

Brest

Continue along the D788 into Brest, the capital, which occupies one of the finest natural harbours in the world — 60 square miles of deep anchorage, linked to the raging Atlantic. Unfortunately, its excellent strategic position and its submarine base was of great assistance to Germany in the last war. From here, they could interfere with convoys sailing between America and Britain. Thus the city suffered heavy bombing and bombardment by the allies. The effect of this, added to the Germans destroying the town centre before the Americans moved in, was widespread devastation.

Brest has subsequently been rebuilt and is now a fine, modern well-planned city with good shops, boulevards and parks, but alas there is not much to see which is of interest to tourists. Weather permitting you will get a good view of the Brest roadstead from Cours Dajot, a promenade laid out in the ramparts by prisoners in 1769. To find out more, visit the museum of Old Brest in Tour Tanguy (16th-century).

Île d'Ouessant

The harbour is Brest's busy focal point. You can take a guided tour around the naval base or a boat trip around the harbour to Le Conquet and Île d'Ouessant (or Ushant island), which can be rough. Although bleak, Ouessant is one of the warmest places in France in winter. About 15 sq. miles altogether, the main settlement is at Lampaul. The isle is renowned for its shellfish and salt mutton, and has always been a staging post for sailors and birds.

The simplest way to explore the island is to hire a bike or a horse. Its terrain is flattish, crisscrossed by dry stone walls, its landscape dotted with grey houses. Life here is basic. Winter is harsh, often sinister when mournfully howling foghorns mingle with the roar of the sea. Most of the people work on the land (only about a tenth of it can be cultivated) or fish. Small brown sheep crop the salty pastures, also some dairy cattle. Because women play such an important role in the island's life, they are traditionally allowed the privilege of proposing marriage.

Closer to land the boat stops at the small Île de Molène (less than a mile long and half a mile wide). Here the isolated community lives by fishing: from May to September they harvest the seaweed. It is a tranquil little place with some good walks.

There are also boat trips from Brest to the island of Sein, off Pointe du Raz, and the Crozon peninsula.

Leaving Brest, drive over Pont Louppe (N165), a modern bridge spanning the Élorn, to the Plougastel peninsula. The chief town, Plougastel-Daoulas, is not very interesting, but remains famous as the centre of a strawberry-growing area, also for its church calvary, one of the most elaborate and celebrated in Brittany. Adorned with 180 figures, it was built 1602–1604 to commemorate the end of the great plague in 1598. The pardon of La Fontaine-Blanche is held on 15 August.

Turning north at Daoulas (D770/712), follow the scenic valley of the Élorn and on to Guimiliau (D111). Guimiliau possesses one of the largest and most famous calvaries (1581–1588) in Brittany: over 200 figures adorn it. Its church (early 17th-century) Flamboyant-Renaissance, has a remarkable south porch, also baptistery. There was — and still is — considerable rivalry between Guimiliau and St-Thégonnec (D712) to outdo each other. It is difficult to say which is the better of the two.

St-Thégonnec's calvary, erected in 1610, tells the tale of Christ's trial, crucifixion and redemption. Its church is fascinating inside, especially its exquisitely-carved wooden pulpit, fit for a Pope. The ossuary has been turned into an ornate and magnificent chapel.

Dinner and overnight at Morlaix.

Castel Régis
Plage Garo
Brignogan-Plages
Tel: 98 83 40 22

Closed:	End of September to Easter, and Wednesday evenings
Facilities:	A garden with tennis and swimming for the active
Rating:	★★★

USEFUL INFORMATION: BRIGNOGAN-PLAGES

Tourist Office:	Rue Général-de-Gaulle
	Tel: 98 83 41 08
Population:	881

USEFUL INFORMATION: BREST

Tourist Office:	1 Place de la Liberté
	Tel: 98 44 24 96
Population:	160,355

Quimper

DAY 4

Morlaix to Quimper: approx. 140 miles.

In the morning the Monts d'Arrée are waiting to be explored — Brittany's highest mountain range where austere crags give way to wooded copses surrounding small hamlets. The whole stands within the protected confines of Armorique Regional Park. Then we continue west to the Crozon peninsula and lunch at Camaret. Here the climate is instantly warmer, and the vegetation is noticeably very different to that of the morning — mediterranean plants can be seen in the village gardens. Leaving Crozon we turn south for dinner at Quimper.

Breakfast at Morlaix.

The scenic D769 gradually winds into the mountains south of Morlaix. The Monts d'Arrée are Brittany's highest mountain range. They were once much higher, but have gradually been eroded over the centuries into rounded hills (Menez) or sharp, fretted, rock crests (roc'h), sometimes wooded, more often covered by heathland.

It is well worth spending some time in the region before setting off for the Crozon peninsula. The Monts d'Arrée part of the Armorique Regional Park is carefully administered so as to allow the visitor to enjoy and appreciate the ecological balance between the natural beauty of the area and the rural industries pursued by the small population. I recommend that you first visit one of the local tourist offices and get a listing of what is available in the park at the time of your visit. There are prepared itineraries for nature walks, horse rides — you can even take a gypsy caravan if feeling nostalgic.

Huelgoat

One way of exploring the park would be to drive first to Huelgoat (D14), which is not particularly interesting for itself but a walk through its hilly wooded Argoat, cut by underground streams and sunken waterways, strewn with boulders and rocks, is well worth doing. Obtain a map from the local tourist office — and follow Rue Cendre as far as Café du Chaos, then take the path to Chaos du Moulin.

Huelgoat is not far from Carhaix, an important town in Roman times, now the centre of a cattle-breeding district, and also a good centre for starting on a tour of the Black Mountains further south.

Nearby at Brennilis and Loqueffret you can admire the remarkable work of a beaver colony (introduced in 1969 and thriving).

From Huelgoat go north past Roc'h Trévézel (D764/785) past Montaigne St Michel to St-Rivoal. (At the foot of Mont-St-Michel-de-Brasparts is a large crafts museum with over 250 exhibitors.) In St-Rivoal you can visit the Maison Cornec, preserved as an example of the local building style in the 17th to 19th centuries. At Ménez-Meur there is a fascinating horse museum, illustrating the importance of horses in Breton society.

Detour

Continue on the D764 past Commana. In a valley between Commana and Sizun lies the village of Les Moulins de Kerouat, built around a waterfall. Here are two water mills, a miller's house with traditional furnishings, and a tannery. At Sizun a watermill has been converted into the Maison de la Rivière de l'Eau at de la Pêche. This is a major educational and research project centring on the importance of water purity. Open to the public, the exhibits here are quite fascinating in particular those focussed on angling.

From St-Rivoal continue along the D42/18 through the forest of Cranou to Le Faou, where you stand on the border of the Crozon peninsula. Le Faou was once a prosperous port but although a few 16th-century houses and a church (note balconied bell tower) remain, it is more rewarding to drive on to Landévennec (D791/60). This is a pretty little resort with a small harbour and the ruins of a Bénédictine Abbey. The abbey is the oldest in Brittany, founded by St Guénolé. The original 5th-century church was destroyed and rebuilt many times. The ruins contain a tomb thought to be that of King Gradlon of Cornwall from the legends of Ys.

Cross the peninsula (D791/887/8) to Camaret for lunch.

Lunch at Hôtel de France, Camaret.

Camaret is yet another pleasant resort in the north-west, and France's most important lobster port. Whitewashed houses are set attractively round the harbour. Boats to Le Conquet, Ouessant, and Tas-de-Pois (rocks on Pen-hir Point) can be taken from here. To be seen in the town is the chapel Notre-Dame du Roc'h Amadour, truly maritime, containing a sailing boat, a fleet of model steamers, anchors, lifebelts and oars. Its redbrick tower contains a nautical museum. The nearest beach on the other side of the sea wall is rather small and is sand and shingle. The ones at Veryach and Kerloc'h are one to two miles away. From Camaret, there is a good walk to Penhir point (about 4½ miles return), in a magnificent setting and with a grand panoramic view.

The Crozon peninsula, jutting out between the Abers in the north and Cornouaille in the south, with its rugged rocky coastline, and steep cliffs, bays, reefs and magnificent views, is Breton seascape at its best. Inland is wild and wooded with frequent stretches of ferns and gorse. However as local transport is rather sketchy a car is vital for exploring its interior, coast and high points. Or, you *must* enjoy long walks. Bathers should beware of treacherous currents, and heed notices.

Morgat

From Camaret on the D355 you can circle the northern tip of the peninsula via Espagnol Point and continue west to Pen-hir Point. Cross back inland (D8/887) to Morgat, the peninsula's best known resort which was once a sardine port. It is situated around a bay, amid rocky cliffs and pines, with a long stretch of beach. Morgat's particular speciality is its caves, some of which can be reached on foot at low tide; others by boat.

The boat trips last about 45 minutes and conduct you through an interesting small network of caves. Ste Marine Cave gained its name from the legend of a girl from Ireland, apparently shipwrecked nearby, who made the cave her home and lived here as a religious hermit until her death. She has been venerated by local fishermen and sailors ever since and is said to help those who call upon her from being wrecked on the rocks. Among the caves there is also the Devil's Chimney, the Devil's Waiting Room and the largest, the Autun Cave (approx. 220ft deep).

You can take a boat from Morgat, incidentally, to the island of Sein.

Crozon

Crozon, the main town and administrative centre, has given its name to this peninsula. It is plain, grey and homespun, dominated by a long church, which contains a celebrated, if rather mysterious reredos, dedicated to the martyrdom of 10,000 Christians, Theban soldiers, who died for their faith during the reign of the Emperor Hadrian. Nobody seems to know why it is there.

From Crozon drive eastwards on D887, to Châteaulin a good excursion centre for Pleyben (largest calvary (1555–1650) in Brittany, and church) and Monts d'Arrée. You pass Ménez Hom, Brittany's highest 'mountain', the top of which can be reached by car. From it are magnificent views back over the Crozon peninsula, also Cornouaille and its capital, Quimper.

Châteaulin spreads across the banks of the Aulne in the heart of an extremely attractive valley. The town is primarily famous for salmon-fishing — there is even a salmon on the Châteaulin coat of arms. Taking the small D770 down to Quimper you will pass the village of St-Venec which boasts a 16th-century calvary, gothic chapel and five fountains. A couple of miles further on Quilinen is a worthwhile stopping place for here there is an even more striking calvary built at the same time.

Southern Finistère

The old Cornouaille (the French Cornwall), once the kingdom and duchy of medieval Brittany, extended further to the west and east. Today it is made up of the rocky head south of Douarnenez and extends to the west of its old capital, Quimper. It is a maritime region with a quiet, cultivated (mainly potatoes and early vegetables) interior.

Quimper

Like Morlaix, Quimper is a town of the past which should be wandered through on foot. Situated in a pretty little valley, it is quite an elegant town compared to most of Brittany's rather plain ones. Its name means 'Confluence', for two rivers, the Odet, sluggish yet dignified, and the Steir, lively and less formal, meet here, cutting through the town in opposite directions.

Quimper's particular pride is its cathedral, St-Corentin (13th- to 15th-century, but two slender towers were erected in 1856), named after its first Bishop, the adviser of the good king Gradlon, who after the destruction by sea of his legendary town of Ys, made Quimper his capital. You can see him riding his granite horse on high between the cathedral's two towers.

While here, you should visit the Fine Arts museum, which contains a good collection of paintings, including Breton landscapes; the Musée Breton devoted to the archeology, history and folklore of the region; pottery workshops and old timber-framed houses and cobbled streets.

Quimper has a traditional Breton atmosphere, and if you're here on the 4th Sunday in July, you will see the great festival of Cornouaille, when old Breton costumes are worn. Quimper is a good centre for excursions; trains, special bus-excursions over Brittany (July/August), local buses, and boat trips.

Dinner and overnight at Tour d'Auvergne, Quimper.

Hôtel de France
sur le port
29129 Camaret-sur-Mer
Tel: 98 27 93 06

Right on the waterfront, the dining room looks straight out over the boats moored in the port.

Closed:	11 November to 1 April
Rooms:	40
Facilities:	Restaurant
Credit cards:	Eurocard, Carte Bleu, American Express, Diners Club
Food:	Live lobster and langoustines. Very varied menu, plenty of meat dishes as well as fish and seafood.
Rating:	★★

USEFUL INFORMATION: CAMARET-SUR-MER

Tourist Office:	Place Charles de Gaulle
	Tel: 98 27 93 60
Population:	3,069

Tour d'Auvergne
13 rue Réguaires
Quimper
Tel: 98 95 08 70

Closed:	19 December to 18 January
Rooms:	45
Credit cards:	American Express, Visa
Rating:	★★★

Hôtel Ibis
Rue G. Eiffel
Quimper
Tel: 98 90 53 80

Open all year
Rooms: 72
Credit cards: Eurocard, Visa
Rating: ★★

Restaurants only:

Le Capucin Gourmand
29 rue Réguaires
Quimper
Tel: 98 95 43 12

Closed: Mid-July to mid-August, Saturday midday and Sundays
Credit cards: Eurocard, Visa
Rating: ★★★

La Rotunde
36 avenue France Libre
Quimper
Tel: 98 95 09 26

Closed: 24 June to 15 July, February, Saturday midday and
                   Sundays
Credit cards: Eurocard, Visa
Rating: ★★

USEFUL INFORMATION: QUIMPER

Tourist Office: 34 rue Douarnenez
                   Tel: 98 53 72 72
Population: 60,162
Amenities: Golf, small airfield

Île de Sein

DAY 5

Quimper to Raz Pointe to Quimper: approx. 105 miles.

Quimper is an excellent centre for discovering the flavour of Cornouaille, the jaw of the dragon. To circle the peninsula anti-clockwise, leave Quimper northwards for the old weaving town of Locronan and then turn west to the picturesque little port of Douarnenez. After the desolate grandeur of Raz Pointe on to a relaxed lunch by the beaches of Audierne. From Audierne you can take a boat to the Île de Sein for the afternoon before returning to Quimper, or you may prefer to remain on the mainland and explore the rather desolate Penmarch peninsula as far as Pont-l'Abbé before driving back to Quimper for a second night.

Breakfast at Quimper.

A popular excursion from Quimper is the one around Cornouaille's rocky indented coast.

Locronan

Locronan, to the north (D39/63), was once known as the city of weavers, now it is a picturesque village, set between forests on a steep hill. Quaint, grey granite, Renaissance-style houses, an old well, and a large church with pretty adjoining chapel, Le Pénity (15th- to 16th-century) with noteworthy carvings and stained-glass windows, stand around a large cobbled square. The church includes a carved and painted pulpit telling stories about St Ronan, the town's namesake, and also his black granite tomb. St Ronan, an Irish hermit, evangelised this corner of Brittany in the 5th century. In particular, he walked 3 miles barefoot every day, and on Sundays, 7 miles. In memory of this, a *Troménie* takes place here each year (2nd Sunday in July), when a procession retraces his steps. A *Grande Troménie* is celebrated every six years, going round the hill for seven miles, halting at 12 points, where parishes display their saints and relics. The journey follows the boundary of the 11th-century Bénédictine Priory (a place of retreat) thus 'Tro Minihy' (a tour of the retreat). Locronan made its wealth by the manufacture of sailcloth. Today it relies on tourism. At nearby Ste-Anne-le-Palud (D63/61), the most colourful of all pardons is celebrated on the last Sunday of August.

Next comes Douarnenez-Tréboul (D107), amalgamated with Ploaré and Pouldavid lying either side of the Pouldavid estuary. Douarnenez was once particularly noted for its sardines; nowadays its catch is more diversified. It has grown considerably from its original size: the most picturesque part is around the quays and old streets of the fishing harbour Tréboul. According to local legend, King Mark, uncle of Tristan, had his palace at Douarnenez and so the island at the mouth of the Pouldavid estuary is named after Tristan. The Feast of the Seagulls and the Blessing of the Sea take place at Douarnenez on the 3rd Sunday of July.

Cap Sizun (D7) incorporates a bird sanctuary (Cap Beuzec) on rocky cliffs, a wild windy place, on to Brézellec Pointe with good views of the coastline, then Pointe du Van (15th-century chapel and a good viewpoint of harsh end-of-the-world-type scenery) and finally Raz Pointe.

Raz Pointe

To stand on Raz Pointe, this high granite spur, is to feel that you really are at the end of the world; the old world, that is. Behind lies France and the continent of Europe. Beyond and around is foaming sea. You can venture along the Pointe on your own but beware of the mists which roll up suddenly without warning and disappear again as quickly. High winds are another hazard. People have been blown off Raz Pointe. A guided tour (about 1½ hrs) reveals spectacles of shattered red rock walls and fissures, against which waves explode in showers of spume; also abysses, such as the Enfer de Plogoff, a Breton hell hole, into which the raging sea continually plunges and fumes.

Between Raz Pointe and the Pointe du Van lies the curving sandy Baie des Trépassés, Bay of the Dead, which supposedly obtained its name because it was here that those drowned along this coast were washed up by the treacherous currents between the island of Sein and the mainland. Or, it may have been because it was here that the dead bodies of druids were brought to be rowed over to the island of Sein for burial.

Île du Sein

But Raz Pointe is not quite the end of France for flat, treeless Sein, less than a mile square in area, lies beyond. Sein's inhabitants remained pagan until the 18th century, and were notorious for living by looting ships wrecked on the rocks, using what they found to furnish their homes. Today, although there are a few tiny fields, the islanders' main livelihood is catching and selling lobsters. It is a galiant little place. In 1940, all the men (130) escaped to England to join de Gaulle's Free French army, and some 3,000 soldiers and sailors embarked from here to England. In 1946, de Gaulle awarded the island the Liberation Cross of Lorraine. A granite memorial commemorates this event and those who died for their country's freedom.

As you walk around the little grey stone houses note the double-topped coiffe worn by a number of the older women. The style was adopted at the beginning of the century when the island population was swept by an epidemic. Now it has become the accepted symbol of bereavement.

There is a ferry boat to Sein from Bestrées, a tiny picturesque port on the southern side of Raz Pointe. It can also be reached from Ste-Evette by the pretty village resort Audierne (D784), on the Goyen Estuary. The trip takes 70 minutes, there are 3 boats a day. To see at Audierne is La Chaumière, a thatched cottage, containing 17th- and 18th-century Breton furniture. Audierne also has a superb expanse of sandy beach. Although its low-lying coast is battered by strong Atlantic waves this has not discouraged fish. Fishponds hold quantities of crustaceans. Audierne has 19 canneries. Numerous pardons are held at Audierne in July and August.

Lunch at Hôtel au Roi Gradlon, Audierne.

From Plozévet, you can return direct to Quimper (D784), or via the Penmarch peninsula, the Bigouden country, where local women sometimes wear a coiffe in the shape of a little lace menhir. In contrast to the steep indented coastline of Cap Sizun, the low-lying Penmarch peninsula sweeps round in a circular bay — there are no harbours. Waves pound down on to rocks. The powerful Eckmühl lighthouse stands at the extreme end of the headland.

Penmarch was once a wealthy region, but in the 16th century, cod, its mainstay, deserted its coastal waters; there was a devastating tidal wave, and the disturbances caused by a rebellion against the Duke of Mercoeur, enabled a brigand called La Fontanelle, to terrorize the countryside. He eventually received his deserts, but the region never quite recovered from all these disasters.

Penmarch Tréoultré (D2/57) is the main centre of the region. St-Guénolé is a quiet pleasant little resort and fishing port on the rather desolate peninsula. It has a small prehistoric museum, while '15th-century Notre-Dame-de-Tronoën is not far from here, set on windswept dunes. Its calvary, dating from the end of the 15th century, is the oldest in Brittany. Pointe de Penmarch is a beautiful spot to stop and admire the scenery.

Loctudy (D53), at the mouth of Pont-l'Abbé river, is a small lively resort and fishing port, with several beaches, a 12th-century church (one of the best preserved Romanesque ones in Brittany), and is not far from Kérazan castle (a gracious manor home, dating from the 16th century). It is open to the public and houses a major collection of paintings and drawings from the 15th century to the present day. Pont-l'Abbé (D2), which stands at the head of the estuary, gets its name from the bridge built by the monks of Loctudy, between the harbour and Étang. It is the capital of the Bigouden region. Apart from market gardening, its speciality is embroidery and making little dolls dressed in the traditional style of the different French provinces. There is an interesting local costume museum in the old castle.

Return to Quimper, D785.

Dinner and overnight at Tour d'Auvergne, Quimper.

Hôtel au Roi Gradlon
29113 Audierne
Tel: 98 70 04 51

The water practically laps at the foot of the terrace. You cannot get closer to the sea. Very reasonable food.

Closed:	5 January to 14 March, and on Mondays
Rooms:	20
Facilities:	Restaurant
Credit cards:	Visa, American Express, Eurocard
Food:	Naturally seafood and fish are their speciality.
Rating:	★★★

USEFUL INFORMATION: AUDIERNE

Tourist Office:	Place de la Liberté
	Tel: 98 70 12 20
Population:	3,094

Concarneau, Ville Close

DAY 6

Quimper to Lorient: approx. 70 miles.

Leaving Quimper through the Odet river valley, we pass through the smart, modern resort of Bénodet and then on to the Fouesnant, an extremely popular area for tourists. This holiday region is a combination of little hamlets, apple orchards, woodland, beaches and sea, linked by country lanes, most pleasant to wander through. The best cider in Brittany comes from this region.

Concarneau's medieval *ville close* offers a very different picture of Brittany before continuing onward to Pont-Aven for lunch. Gauguin's association with Pont-Aven is well-known and the town's museum should definitely be visited. After a short stop at Quimperlé the route heads eastwards to Lorient.

Breakfast at Quimper.

Travelling southwards you can either drive down the D34 to Bénodet or you can take a trip from Quimper down the Odet river, one of France's prettiest waterways, a winding 15 miles' journey through a surprisingly varied countryside. Sometimes it widens into lake-like size, verging into marshlands; sometimes it is secretly narrow, hemmed in by thick vegetation. Many châteaux and manors were built on the lush meadows beside it. Bénodet, at its mouth, is also pretty, and a lively, smartish (for Brittany) resort, very popular as a sailing centre. From here you can take a boat to Loctudy and the Glénan isles, an archipelago of nine islets, renowned for their sailing school, skin-diving, bird sanctuaries, as well as for wild ponies.

This region of Finistère, between the river Odet and Le Fouesnant, is one of the favourite places in Brittany for camping, sailing and family holidays. Its Cornish-type coastline is made up of innumerable secluded caves, where sheltering pines line stretches of white sands, bordering a calm sea. Inland, winding roads (often called '*hents*') twist through woodlands or hamlets of typical, whitewashed, grey-slate roofed Breton houses. There are plenty of camp sites to choose from — I know, as I have camped here myself — but avoid July and August, when French holidaymakers descend. June and September are pleasantly uncrowded months.

Just south of Bénodet (D44/134) is Mousterlin with a small harbour and an enormous expanse of white sand, the Mer Blanche. Fouesnant inland on the D145 produces the best Breton cider of all. It has an interesting 12th-century church (partly rebuilt in the 18th century) and colourful Friday market. Local costumes and headdresses are worn at the Feast of the Apple Trees and at the Pardon of Ste-Anne (26th July or the following Sunday). Beg Meil (D45) at the entrance to La Forêt Bay, although a small resort, has some superb beaches — two small ones either side of the Cale (the jetty) and those of the dunes looking out across the bay to the Isles of Glénan. In season, you can take a boat here to the Glénan Isles, up the Odet river, and to Concarneau, on the opposite side of the bay.

Continuing along the D44, La Forêt Fouesnant, a village grown into a town, is situated at the head of a creek, La Forêt Bay, surrounded by woods, amid a cider apple region. Plage de Kerleven, about a mile away, is the nearest beach.

Concarneau

Take the D783 to Concarneau, France's third largest fishing port, a busy sailing centre and resort. Its name originates from the Breton 'Conk Kernie' (port of Cornouaille). Concarneau's chief attraction is its Ville Close, a walled town on an islet in the harbour, connected to the mainland by bridges. One enters by way of a medieval arch, part of the old fortifications, and it takes about half an hour to stroll through the narrow cobbled alleys, catching occasional glimpses of the sea and ships through loopholes and archways leading out on to tiny quaysides. You can walk round its 14th-century ramparts and visit the Fishing Museum (Musée de la Pêche) in what was once an arsenal. Notices, models, photos, dioramas tell the history of the town, its evolution as a port and its fishing industry. There is also a shell museum while a marinarium exhibiting the flora and fauna of the sea is in the new town. Although strengthened and added to by Vauban in the 17th century, Ville Close dates back to the 14th century and has withstood attacks made by both the English and the Huguenots.

The town's best beaches — Plages des Sables Blanc — lie westward beyond Pointe de Croix. On the other side is Cabellou Plage, rather small but in a sheltered bay. From Cabellou Pointe are some good views of Concarneau, La Forêt Bay and the coastline.

When here visit the fish auction where the town's wide variety of fish — some you probably won't recognise — are laid out in the covered market. Activity never ceases on the quaysides; here the fish soups are tempting and there is always something new to watch. Although Concarneau has had to adapt to new techniques, thus losing some local colour, the memory of its long fishing history is retained in its Filets Bleus Festival (Blue Nets Festival) — folk dancing and processions — held on the last Sunday but one in August. The first fête was held in 1905 in aid of the sardine fishermen and their families.

Take the D783 to Pont-Aven.

Detour

Just before Pont-Aven you could turn down to Névez and the left bank of the Aven. Here you can wander through sunken country lanes with white-washed thatched cottages. From the sandy beach at Port-Manech there is a footpath up the Aven banks to the port of Kerdruc and thence to the Château of Henan (tidal water mill and pond). The local specialities are crêpes, fish of all varieties and, of course, cider.

Pont-Aven

Pont-Aven is an inland town, tucked in between hills, where the river opens out into an estuary in a green wooded valley. Alas, not many of the famous windmills remain — there were once fourteen — whose picturesqueness drew many artists here. Cheap accommodation was probably another attraction. Even so, artists still come, especially admirers of Gauguin and his disciples. The Pont-Aven school was the designation for the young exponents of Synthetism, headed by Paul Gauguin and Émile Bernard in the 1880's. Gauguin and his followers tried to emulate the simple rustic and superstitious life of the Breton peasants and painted the everyday doings of ordinary people around them. That the Pont-Aven school did not evolve into an artistic and communal school was because Gauguin decided to continue his pursuit of the primitive in Tahiti. But it did lead to a revival of religious painting for which Maurice Denis was one of the chief exponents. Gauguin's works are sometimes shown in the Pont-Aven museum near the Town Hall.

Lunch at Pont-Aven at the Hôtellerie le Moulin de Rosmadec.

In Pont-Aven you can take a leisurely walk through the Bois d'Amour, the riverside woods to the north of the town which provided the inspiration for many of the Pont-Aven artists of the last century. A Gorse Bloom Festival (Fête des Fleurs d'Ajoncs), instigated by poet, song-writer and singer, Théodore Botrel, who spent much of his life here, is held on the first Sunday in August.

All around this area is delightful. Take the D24 to cross the Bélon river, which joins the Aven at the sea. The Bélon is famous for oysters (called Bélons and flat-shaped, now farmed in other places too). Note, as you drive through Moëlan-sur-Mer and its surrounds, the menhirs which dot the landscape varying from 3–15ft in height. Some say the town's name is derived from an early sacred sight called by the Romans *Medislanum*; an alternative version holds that an Irish monk, Moë, had a hermitage (*lan* in Breton) here. Continue past Carnoët zoo and le Pouldu, Gauguin's seaside home. Turning inland, keep to the river valley (D49) through attractive woodland to Quimperlé at the junction of the Ellé and Isole rivers. The old quarter, with protruding upper storeys of the ancient houses, surrounds the Ste-Croix church (12th-century, rebuilt 19th-century).

Morbihan

This south-east corner of Brittany takes its name from its great lake, the gulf of Morbihan, which means 'little sea'. There are innumerable large sandy beaches along its Atlantic coastline, which is warmer and less indented than that of the north. Fishing and oyster breeding are important industries. Inland are many rivers, woodlands and lakes, also megaliths, chapels, castles and manors. As the land is not very fertile, it is used chiefly for cattle-rearing, dairy-production and cider-orchards. All in all, the Morbihan is considered to be a poor and rather backward area of France.

Lorient

From Quimperlé take the N265/165 to Lorient, an important naval base, dockyard and commercial port. Lorient obtained its name because its 17th-century business was confined to India and China — ships based at Le Havre were too easily captured by the English in the channel. Unfortunately, like so many other French ports, it was devastated during the last war, so what you will see there today is a new city built on spacious lines, quite unlike the old.

Lorient was founded by the French East India Company and so an interesting collection of porcelain from the Company is displayed at the naval museum (housed in a 17th-century powder mill).

Dinner and overnight at Le Bretagne, Lorient.

le Moulin de Rosmadec
29123 Pont-Aven
Tel: 98 06 00 22

Very atmospheric, fifteenth-century stone mill building. Terraces overlook racing mill streams and placid mill ponds, outside and inside splendid beamed ceilings and big stone fireplaces.

Closed:	Wednesdays
Rooms:	4
Credit cards:	Visa
Food:	Suprême de sole au champagne, Aiguillettes de canard au cassis and even Homard grillé Rosmadec are considered the high points of their menus.
Rating:	★★★

USEFUL INFORMATION: CONCARNEAU

Tourist Office:	Quai d'Aiguillon
	Tel: 98 97 01 44
Population:	18,225

USEFUL INFORMATION: LORIENT

Tourist Office:	Place Jules-Ferry
	Tel: 97 21 07 84
Population:	64,675

Le Bretagne
6 place Libération
Lorient
Tel: 97 64 34 65

Closed:	21 December to 17 January and Sundays
Rooms:	34
Credit cards:	American Express, Diners, Eurocard, Visa
Rating:	★★★

Hôtel Arvor
104 rue L. Carnot
Lorient
Tel: 97 21 07 55

Closed:	20 December to 5 January and Sundays
Rooms:	20
Rating:	★★

For good food and wine try:

Le Cornouaille
13 boulevard Maréchal Franchet-d'Esperey
Lorient
Tel: 97 21 23 05

Closed:	July and Sundays
Credit cards:	American Express, Diners, Eurocard, Visa
Rating:	★★

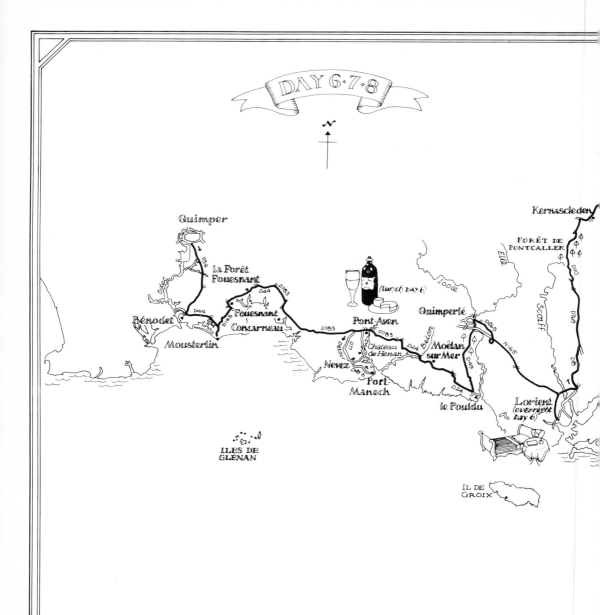

DAY 6·7·8

N

Quimper

Kernascleden

FORÊT DE
PONTCALLEK

la Forêt
Fouesnant

Bénodet

Fouesnant
Concarneau

Mousterlin

(lunch DAY 6)

Quimperlé

Pont-Aven

Chateau
de Henan

Moëlan
sur Mer

Nevez

Port-
Manech

le Pouldu

Lorient
(overnight
Day 6)

ILES DE
GLÉNAN

IL DE
GROIX

GROTTE
l'APOTHICAIRE

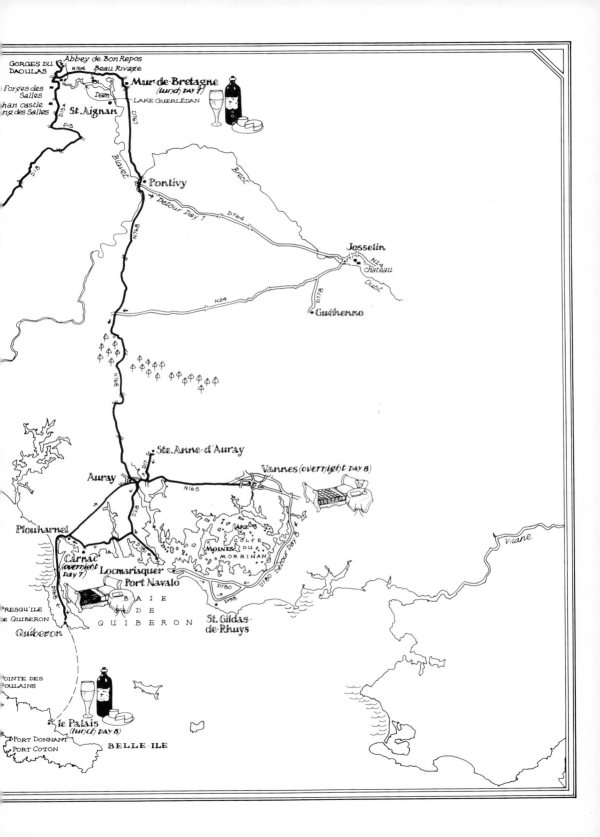

Menhirs at Carnac

DAY 7

Lorient to Carnac: approx. 110 miles.

Leaving Lorient the route heads inland for a morning at the Lac de Guerlédan — a vast man-made lake in the midst of the Quénécan Forest. Here there is much to see, from the romantic beauty of the ruins of Bon Repos to the splendour of the Gorges de Daoulas. After lunch at Mur-de-Bretagne we head past Pontivy to the ancient town of Auray, and thence to spend the afternoon amid the megaliths of Carnac.

Breakfast at Lorient.

Travel north (D18/769/110) through the Forêt de Pontcallec to Kernascléden.

Kernascléden is only a small village but it possesses a large and very beautiful church, famous among Breton churches for the perfection of its detail, which although of exquisite delicacy does not overload or distract from the whole. To note especially are the statues of the apostles in the left porch and the 15th-century frescoes, representing episodes in the life of the Virgin and Christ, and the vault and walls surmounting the main arches. Don't miss the fragmented dance of death on the walls of the south arm. Here is a graphic picture of hell, where the damned undergo such horrors as being impaled, roasted and boiled.

Lac de Guerlédan

Continue north (D782/18) to approach the huge artificial Lac de Guerlédan through the Quénécan forest. This area of water, woods and hills is sometimes known as Suisse Breton. There is much to see and do in the area, all is centred on the lake — over 12 miles long — which stretches between Gouarec and Mur-de-Bretagne. The lake is fed by the Nantes–Brest canal, and is held back by the Guerlédan Dam between St-Aignan and Mur-de-Bretagne at the eastern end. The lake was built in 1924–29, and the waters engulfed 17 locks, and the lock-keepers' houses.

In the route I suggest below we approach the lake from the southwestern edge, then crossing the canal at Bon Repos, travel along the northern bank of the lake to Mur-de-Bretagne. I strongly recommend that you leave your car and walk as much as possible in this invigorating area.

Les Forges des Salles (D15, 15a) and the Château de Forges is situated amid deep green oak and beech groves. Just before Les Forges the road passes the small Étang des Salles overlooked by the romantic ruins of Rohan Castle. The 12th-century Abbey of Bon Repos lies north of Les Forges over an ancient stone bridge, just before the Gorges de Daoulas (D44). Here the river has cut deeply and dramatically into the rocks as the valley winds and twists through scrublands of gorse and heather.

Mur-de-Bretagne

Mur-de-Bretagne (N164/D767) is an excellent stopping place. The shores of the lake here are crisscrossed with forest walks. The huge dam lies just south of the village. Before you begin exploring the tracks around the lake I suggest you collect some detailed information on possible walks from the Mur-de-Bretagne Tourist Office, whose staff are extremely helpful.

If you are feeling leisurely and wish to sightsee while you eat you can take a restaurant-boat from Beau Rivage (on the lake shore south of Caurel, off N164), and eat whilst cruising around the lake.

Otherwise, lunch at Auberge Grand Maison, Mur-de-Bretagne.

Obviously the lake provides a variety of fresh fish but here savoury galettes (buckwheat pancakes) are a local speciality; with eggs, cheese and ham a galette is a meal in itself.

Leave Mur-de-Bretagne on the D767 southwards, beside the winding canal, to Pontivy.

Pontivy

Pontivy, beside the Blavet, is a central market-town and good excursion centre, linking as it does with the Montagnes Noires and places of interest, such as Vannes, Josselin and Guerlédan lake. It is an interesting mixture of centuries. Narrow winding streets recalling medieval times contrast with the geometrical town laid out by Napoleon. During the Napoleonic Wars, Napoleon decided to build a canal connecting Brest with Nantes. As Pontivy lay about halfway, he decided to make it a strategic and military centre, even changing its name to Napoléonville. This was later dropped after the fall of his empire, and was only finally revived again for a period during the reign of Napoléon III.

Detour

Josselin (D764), to the east of Pontivy, is Brittany's most splendid castle. To see it at its fairytale-best — strong walls and tall pointed towers mirrored proudly in the water — you should stand on the bridge over the Oust, coming from Malestroit.

Josselin played an important part in the War of Succession and the Hundred Years' War. Amongst its owners was Oliver de Clisson, who succeeded du Guesclin as Constable of France, and who married Marguerite of Rohan, the widow of Beaumanoir, a previous owner. He strengthened the castle, adding eight towers and a keep. Later dukes of Rohan transformed the castle into a model Renaissance seat, whose regal aspect fully justified their motto, 'I cannot be a king, I scorn to be a prince, I am a Rohan'. And the family still live there today, in what must be one of France's loveliest stately homes.

The old surrounding town is worth strolling round. Some streets have names recalling important local events. You should visit its Notre-Dame-du-Roncier (Our Lady of the Rosebush), founded in the 11th century, and restored and remodelled though the centuries.

Ten miles to the south-west (N24/D778) is the Guéhenno calvary (built 1550, since restored), beautifully-sculptured with representations of the drama of the Passion. In front is a column surmounted by a cock, a reminder of Peter's denial of Christ.

Take the D24/768 to Auray.

Auray

The main route from Pontivy leads south to Auray (N168/D768), an old town at the head of the Loc'h or Auray estuary. Its chief attractions are its harbour and the St-Goustan quarter with its old, half-timbered houses and steep streets. There is a good view of both from the Loc'h Promenade. Americans might be interested to learn that Benjamin Franklin landed on the quay to the left of Place St-Sauveur in 1776. He sailed from Philadelphia to negotiate a treaty with France during the War of Independence against Britain.

Auray played an important part in Breton history, for it was here that the battle which ended the War of Succession was fought in 1364, when Charles de Blois was killed. English-backed John Montfort chivalrously distressed at his rival's death, had him buried with great magnificence near Guingamp, and founded a chapel and church in his honour on the battlefield. After becoming a monastery, it is now a home for deaf and dumb women. The mausoleum in the convent's chapel holds the bones and skulls of 350 exiles and Chouans, who were shot in the nearby Champs des Martyrs, after the ill-fated Quiberon landings. Ste-Anne d'Auray, further inland (D17) was erected in the Renaissance style in the last century. It is Brittany's most important pilgrimage centre. The Pardons of Ste Anne held on 26th July and 15th August are the two most popular in the province. Legend has it that Ste Anne, a woman of noble blood, and mother of the Virgin Mary, came from Cornouaille but was taken to Nazareth by angels to save her from a brutal husband. After the birth of Mary she returned to Brittany where Christ himself is supposed to have visited his grandmother. There is a local saying 'Whether dead or alive every Breton goes at least once to Ste-Anne d'Auray'.

Locmariaquer, on the southwestern peninsula of the gulf (D28, D781), is a pretty village and family resort. Nearby is the Witches' stone, the great menhir (the largest known and broken into 5 pieces) and merchants' table (3 flat granite slabs resting on 17 supports) and Dolmen of Mané Lud.

Carnac

But it is Carnac in the southwest (D781), which is Brittany's most celebrated region of pre-history. Some three thousand menhirs cover the area, the best known being those of Ménec along D196, off the main road just outside Carnac-Ville. Here 1169 upended boulders, all shapes and sizes, stand in rows beside the roadway resembling, if anything, some sort of ancient building site. There are eleven rows, measuring 1260 yards along and 108 yards wide. Their exact purpose and age is still a matter of controversy, but their position in regard to sun and moon at particular times (at equinoxes and solstices) suggest they were once an enormous temple for sun worshippers. A good overall view of them may be had from St-Michel Tumulus (about 1½ miles away) a great mound of earth and stones covering several burial chambers. There is a calvary and chapel on top.

There are other alignments at Kermario (982 menhirs in 10 lines) and Kerlescan (540 menhirs in 13 lines) and the Tumulus of Moustoir, within an area of a few miles. A visit to the little museum at Carnac-Ville should not be missed. Carnac-Ville joins up with Carnac-Plage, a popular tourist resort, with lots of villas and pines and very long sandy beach. Note: on the main beach — Grande Plage — no dogs are allowed. La Trinité-sur-Mer, further east, whose old granite village slopes down to the harbour, one of the best on the Atlantic coast, is a favourite yachting centre. There are boat excursions from here to Belle Île, and the islands of Hoëdic and Houat.

Dinner and overnight at La Marine, Carnac.

Auberge Grand'Maison
1 rue Leas le Cerf
22530 Mur-de-Bretagne
Tel: 96 28 51 10

A varied menu of interesting complex dishes. Jaques Guillo, the owner chef, rules the kitchen and devises many of the dishes. Stylish and elegant surroundings.

Closed:	Sunday evenings and Mondays
Rooms:	15
Credit cards:	All
Food:	'la Marguerite de Saint Jacques, servie tiède, vinaigrette aux herbes fraiches' and 'les Galettes de pommes de terre au saumon fumée en creme froide de caviar' show the style of cuisine.
Rating:	★★★★

USEFUL INFORMATION: MUR-DE-BRETAGNE

Tourist Office:	Place Église
	Tel: 96 28 51 41
Population:	2,165

Hotel Restaurant La Marine
4 Place de la Chapelle
56340 Carnac
Tel: 97 52 07 33

A family-run hotel, very close to the Museum of Prehistory.

Closed: January
Rooms: 33
Facilities: Restaurant
Credit cards: Carte Bleu, Eurocard, Visa, American Express, Diners Club
Food: Seafood and fish the speciality of the house. Cheaper
                 menus available during the week.
Rating: ★★★

USEFUL INFORMATION: CARNAC	
Tourist Office:	74 Avenue Druides
	Tel: 97 52 13 52
Population:	3964
Amenities:	Golf

Vannes

DAY 8

Carnac to Vannes: approx. 45 miles, excluding boat trips.

After a short drive down the narrow strip of land known as the Presqu'ile de Quiberon, we can take a boat to Belle Île — the largest of the Breton islands whose quiet fishing ports, whitewashed houses and beautiful beaches are deceptively peaceful considering its stormy past.

After lunch we return to the mainland to spend the afternoon at Vannes on the Morbihan Gulf. From Vannes you can take a boat trip around the gulf, perhaps stopping at some of the islands. Alternatively you can follow the perimeter of the Gulf and drive down to Rhuys Peninsula and Port-Navalo.

Breakfast at Carnac.

Leave Carnac on the D781 for Plouharnel, a small Breton country town. There are a couple of interesting museums here — the Chouanerie and the Museum of Megaliths. Plouharnel has become increasingly attractive to tourists. Its countryside is dotted with small hamlets, old cottages and now camping sites. Water sports take place from its 3 miles' long, dune-sheltered Sables Blanc beach.

Quiberon Peninsula

Plouharnel lies at the head of the Quiberon peninsula, once an island, now attached to the mainland by a narrow strip of sandy land and dunes, pinned down by pines. Its role is that of a jetty to the bay of Quiberon. On its west side is the Côte Sauvage, rugged and dangerous, facing towards the Atlantic. On the east side and towards the end are the resorts.

In the past Quiberon suffered Viking invasions, also attacks by English, Dutch, German and Portuguese. One famous sea battle, in 1759, was when Admiral Hawke defeated the French fleet under Conflans. The most famous battle of all was the one which took place on one of the beaches when Breton Blues, commanded by Hoche, defeated the Chouans and Emigrés, in 1795. Hoche's statue stands in the town of Quiberon in the little park near the front. An obelisk marks the spot where the invaders surrendered to General Hoche, while the road behind the beach is called Boulevard des Emigrés. The Emigrés had planned to join up with the Chouans, and landings had begun at Carnac-Plage, but they were driven back to the Quiberon peninsula.

The resort of Quiberon at the end of the peninsula has a good beach and climate — a luxurious sanatorium has been established, where seawater cures take place — but it is rather commercialised. From here, you can make trips into the Morbihan gulf and to Belle Île, Houat and Houëdic.

Belle Île

Like Quiberon, Belle Île (9 miles away), about three quarters of an hour by steamer) has a good climate. Approximately 10 miles long and 3–6 miles wide it has a varied countryside. The island's most attractive features are its serenity and its innumerable coves and beautiful beaches. Le Palais, where the steamer stops, is the main town. To see there is its citadel, strengthened by Vauban, which contains an interesting museum, including mementoes of Sarah Bernhardt, and of the two World Wars.

Because of its vulnerable position, Belle Île has had quite a stormy history, and has been attacked many times by British and Dutch fleets. Charles IX gave it to the Duke of Retz in 1572, whose family later sold it to Nicholas Fouquet, Superintendant for Finance of Louis XIV. He became its *seigneur*, built himself a château, then a fleet, hoping perhaps to establish his own private kingdom. His arrest, and subsequent imprisonment, prevented him from completing the islands' fortifications, which were done later by Vauban.

Belle Île is an ideal place for those seeking a peaceful holiday — swimming, sailing, fishing, walking, sunbathing — but is not for those needing sophisticated amusements. There are about 140 'villages' — mere clusters of whitewashed houses. Sauzon is a picturesque fishing port (lobsters and sardines) and sailing centre. Bangor is the oldest. Its church dates from 1071.

Like Quiberon again, Belle Île has its Côte Sauvage on the west side — dangerous for bathing, but where there are some magnificent views; Pointe des Poulains (near where Sarah Bernhardt's château once stood); the Grotte de l'Apothicairerie (the name is derived from cormorants' nests built along the rocky walls, supposed to resemble jars in a chemist's shop); Port Donnant, a very pretty bay; the great lighthouse (whose beam spans forty miles — there is a fine view from the balcony); and Aiguilles de Port Coton (the sea on the reef is supposed to build up like a mass of cotton wool).

Port Andro, on its eastern side, marks the beginning of the Douce, the calm sweet side of the island, where lie the bathing beaches, although Port Kérel in its sheltered setting on the west side, is the most popular.

Lunch at La Forge on Belle-Île.

Return to Quiberon and head for Vannes (D768/N165).

Vannes and the Morbihan Gulf

Vannes, capital of the Morbihan region and an important centre, lies at the head of the Morbihan Gulf. It is a town of sturdy character, friendly yet dignified, its old quarter and cathedral enclosed by ramparts, with flowery gardens to one side. Vannes was the first and last of Brittany's capitals. It was here that Nominoë, Count of Vannes, declared himself ruler of Brittany. Centuries later, in 1532, the Parliament meeting at Vannes, proclaimed the perpetual unity of the County and Duchy of Brittany with the Kingdom and Crown of France.

Start your tour from Place Henri IV, surrounded by 16th-century houses, over which looms the Romanesque tower of St-Pierre (13th- to 19th-century). In the Renaissance chapel (16th-century) in nearby Rue de Chanoines is the tomb of St Vincent Ferrier, a Spanish monk, who came to Vannes to preach. He died here in 1419. It was his evangelising, later maintained by those two 17th-century zealots, Le Nobletz and Maunoir, which led to Brittany's religious fervour and the establishment of so many calvaries, crosses and churches.

In Place des Lices, you will find the 15th-century house of Vannes and his wife, and the city's mascots. Exactly who the merry faces sticking out from a beam are is unknown. There are many conjectures. Almost opposite is the 15th-century Château Gaillard, once the meeting place of Brittany's refugee 'parliament', which was exiled from Rennes by Louis XIV, after their revolt against the Stamp Act. It now houses a prehistoric museum, devoted chiefly to specimens from the Carnac region and a natural science museum.

The best of Vannes lies on its east and south side, where the medieval ramparts and towers set off the 18th-century gardens. In the garden of the Garenne is a memorial to the men killed in the World Wars, also a tablet commemorating those 22 men, including the Bishop of Dol, who were shot here for the part they played in the Quiberon landings The most picturesque corners of Vannes are the washing places that border the stream at the foot of the walls, where washerwomen went about their mundane tasks.

'Morbihan' in Breton meant 'little sea'. The Gulf of Morbihan, about 12 miles wide and 10 miles long, contains innumerable little islands, low flat and wooded, often hidden by mists, at least 40 of which are inhabited. Much boating activity takes place on it during the summer.

The best way to see the Gulf is by boat, which starts from Vannes, but trips can also be made from other places round the gulf — Locmariaquer, Port-Navalo and Auray. The main islands to visit are Arz with its tiny village of Gréavet and beautiful Moines, 3 miles long, the largest of the islands and the most populated. Many Bretons retire to this picturesque and peaceful little paradise renowned for its lush mediterranean vegetation. Even the woods bear poetic names, such as the wood of sighs, the wood of love and the wood of regrets. Moines was given to monks, long since departed, by a Breton king, about 854 AD. You can visit islands individually, stop off at one then continue your journey on another boat, or tour the gulf in one long trip, depending on the time at your disposal.

Detour

You can drive eastwards from Vannes (D780) to Port-Navalo, a fishing and yachting centre, on the Rhuys peninsula which nearly encloses the Gulf of Morbihan in the south. The climate here is mild — there is a mediterranean-type vegetation — and it is the only region in Brittany now where wine is produced (cheap, rough and very intoxicating). Two miles to the east of Port-Navalo is Butte Cesar, the tumulus from which Julius Caesar is supposed to have watched the sea battle between the Romans and Veniti.

The village, St-Gildas-de-Rhuys (D198), owes its name to a monastery founded by St Gildas in the 6th century and which in the 12th century had Abélard (of Abélard and Héloise fame) as its abbot. His search for peace, however, proved unsuccessful, and he was obliged to flee from this savage place. About half a mile away stands solid Suscinio castle (13th-century) which became the summer residence of the Dukes of Brittany and was later used by François I. It also underwent some difficult times. It was badly damaged during the Revolution, losing two of its towers and some of its roofs and floors. Restoration was begun in 1966 but chiefly to preserve what remains of its former glory.

Dinner and overnight at La Marée Bleue, Vannes.

Restaurant La Forge
Route de Goulphar
56360 Belle-Ile-en-Mer
Tel: 97 31 51 76

Sophisticated but not pricey food served in a fresh rustic ambience. The same partnership runs a pâtisserie (les Délices du Palais) where you can take tea and buy cakes of the region.

Closed:	December to 1 April
Credit cards:	Visa, Carte Bleu, Mastercard, American Express
Food:	Moules en croutons, Gratin de homard, Turbot au beurre de cidre and Bavarois au coulis de framboises.
Rating:	★★★

Hôtel Restaurant 'La Marée Bleue'
8 Place Bir-Hakeim
56000 Vannes
Tel: 97 47 24 29

Right in the centre of town.

Closed:	19 December to 5 January
Rooms:	16
Facilities:	Restaurant, car park
Credit cards:	All
Food:	Good value food based on traditional Breton cooking
Rating:	★★

Image Ste-Anne
8 place Libération
Vannes
Tel: 97 63 27 36

Closed:	1 November to end March and Sundays
Rooms:	32
Credit cards:	Visa, Eurocard
Rating:	★★

USEFUL INFORMATION: VANNES

Tourist Office:	1 Rue Thiers
	Tel: 97 47 24 34
Population:	45,397

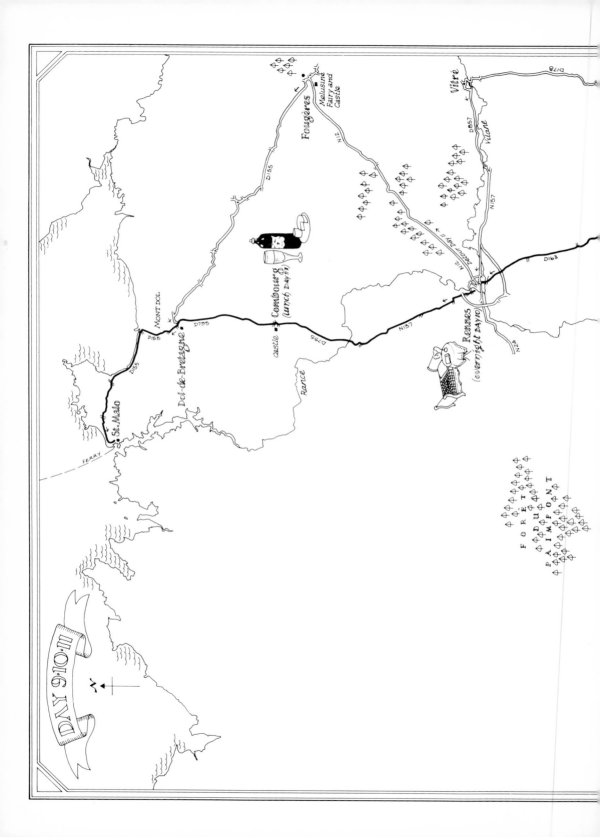

DAY 9·10·11

St. Malo

FERRY

MONT DOL

Dol-de-Bretagne

D155

D155

Rance

Castle

Combourg
(lunch Day 9)

D755

D796

Fougères

Melusiné
Fairy and
Castle

N12

N137

Rennes
(overnight Day 10)

N24

N157

Vitré

Vilaine

D857

D178

D163

FORÊT DU PAIMPONT

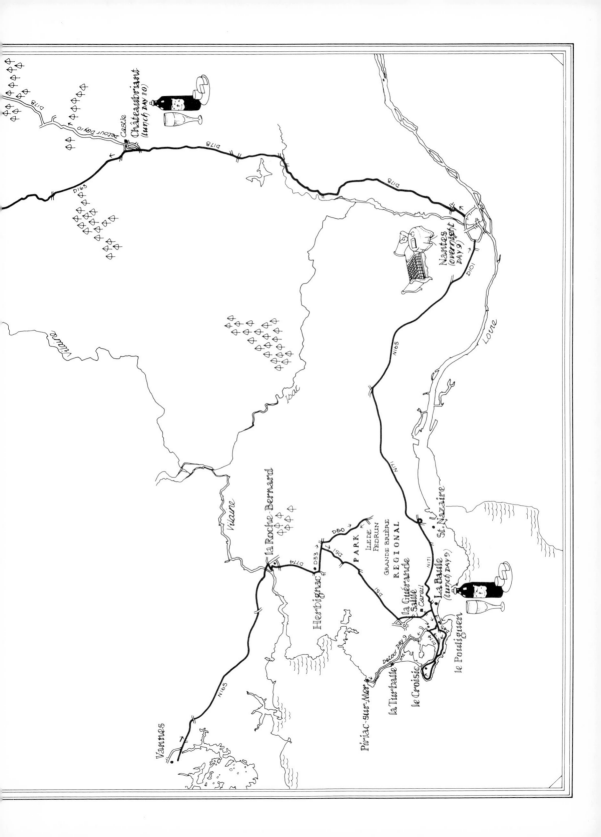

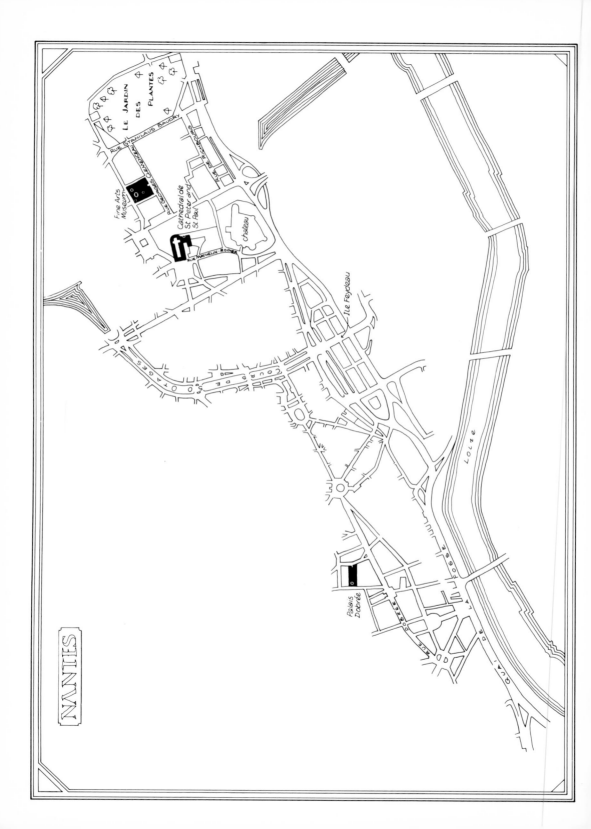

NANTES

LE JARDIN DES PLANTES

RUE STANILAUS BAUDRY

RUE GEORGES CLEMENCEAU

RUE DE RICHEBOURG

Fine Arts Museum

Cathedrale
St Peter and
St Paul

Château

RUE MATHELIN RODIER

Ile Feydeau

LOIRE

COURS DE TOSTAGES

Palais Dobrée

QUAI DE LA FOSSE

DAY 9

Vannes to Nantes: approx. 135 miles.

A day of contrasts — first through the picturesque countryside of the Vilaine to La Grande Brière — a swampy land of water, dark peat bogs and thatched cottages. Standing proud against the skyline is the old walled city of La Guérande, looking out to sea over the salt marshes. Next, to La Baule, sophisticated and smart, for lunch before setting out along the Guérande peninsula, dotted with fishing ports and dominated by the surrounding salt marshes. Leaving the coast we then head for Nantes, Brittany's biggest and busiest city, industrial, maritime, artistic and intellectual, and belonging to both the Breton and French world.

La Baule

Breakfast at Vannes.

Travel south (N165) to La Roche Bernard strategically situated astride the Vilaine, with an old and new harbour and a picturesque cobbled old quarter in the Place du Bouffary and Ruicard Promenade. It makes a fitting gateway to the Loire Atlantique.

Loire-Atlantique or Pays de la Loire

Although Loire-Atlantique is no longer in Brittany and has been incorporated into Pays de la Loire (France was divided into 21 regions in 1964), it fits in best here. It is in this region that the long Loire at last reaches the Atlantic after separating the old Pays de Retz and Vendée from old Brittany. Superb sands, pine groves, a mild climate and Atlantic breezes make it a popular holiday region. Of its scores of resorts, international La Baule is the most famous. Of its cities, Nantes, Brittany's one-time celebrated capital, is the best-known.

The Guérande peninsula and its hinterland contain two contrasting areas, the white country, the salt marsh land around its coast and La Grande Brière, and the black country, where peat bogs lie below inland Grande Brière. Take the D774, D47 to the swampy Grande Brière, lying between the Vilaine and the Loire. It presents a picturesque (especially in spring when covered in flowers) if melancholy picture of islets and pools of water surrounded by reeds, tamarisks and willows. Since 1970, it has been known as the Brière Regional Park, still inhabited by people who, traditionally, punted their way around the canals, lived off the wild life, used peat, and thatched their cottages. Canals have been cleared and old cottage industries encouraged. Tourists can take boat trips on the canals, visit the bird and animal reserve, and drive round the region to the island of Fédrun (D50), surrounded by marshes.

Here, open throughout the summer months, is the Brièreon — a thatched cottage which shows the lifestyle of previous marsh-dwellers. The village of Kerhinet has been completely restored.

Leaving the Grande Brière by the D51 will take you to La Guérande, a walled city, standing on a plateau, overlooking the salt marshes. It is remarkably well-preserved with ramparts almost intact, four fortified gates and old towers. Its site was occupied in prehistoric times. After the fall of the Roman empire, the country here was taken over by Bretons from Britain. A chief, Waroc'h, leader of the Vannetais, conquered the country between the Loire and Vilaine, and erected a baptistery, around which houses were built, the beginning of the town. In 846, the Bishop Gislard, protected by Nominoë, King of Brittany, was installed at Guérlande, which became an episcopal see, in opposition to the Bishop at Nantes. This did not last, but under Salomon, second king of Brittany, the cathedral St-Aubin became a collegiate, with a chapter of canons, which it remained until the Revolution. Guérande is famous in history as the place where Montfort's victory at Auray, ending the War of Succession, was confirmed. The Treaty of Guérande was signed here in 1365. St-Aubin church should be visited as well as an interesting museum in the eastern fortified gateway.

In Roman times the sea lay between the rocky island of Batz and Guérande. A change of level turned the gulf into marshes. Batz became linked with the mainland by the strip on which Le Pouliguen and La Baule now stands. There is a gap between Le Croisic and Penbron point, through which the sea flows at high tide into the old gulf, the Grand and Petit Traicts. At low tide, it becomes an area of mud flats, from which mussels, winkles, clams and oysters are gathered. Other parts of the salt marsh are used for salt pans (marais salants).

Take the D92 towards La Baule. The road passes Careil manor house (14th-century, improved in the 15th and 16th centuries). To see are the 15th-century fireplaces and ceilings, Renaissance furniture and a collection of 17th-century Le Croisic pottery.

La Baule

Stretched out around a magnificent area of coast, La Baule is in the Cannes/ Biarritz class for size and sophistication. Its chief attractions are its climate, its 3-mile (5 kms) sweep of sandy beach and its facilities — sailing, swimming, tennis, golf, riding, horse-racing, casino, cabarets, night-clubs, smart hotels and restaurants. Like other resorts of this type, La Baule is not particularly old, and only dates from 1879. It has simply expanded and expanded, mainly along the coast, westwards to Le Pouliguen (fishing port, yachting port and resort at the mouth of the canal), and eastwards to Pornichet (popular resort and salt-water spa). It is protected from the north wind by acres of maritime pines (residential La-Baule-les-Pins), the west wind by Point Penchâteau and the east wind by Point Chémoulin.

Lunch at L'Espadon, La Baule.

To explore the Guérande peninsula, take the D45 via Le Pouliguen, and skirt Grand coast, whose cliffs and grottoes contrast with the low coast round La Baule. Batz has an interesting church (St-Guénole, 16th-century); Le Croisic as a seaside resort and fishing port is perhaps too commercialised, but has a nice bit of old town, and a 16th-century church.

Return on the D774 via Saillé, a salt village where you can visit the Maison des Paludiers (Salt Marsh Workers' House). The quays are backed by narrow streets of 15th-, 16th- and 17th-century houses.

Detour

If time allows you can take the D92 at Saillé and cross the salt marshes up to La Turballe — a famous sardine port — and on along the coast to Piriac-sur-Mer, which offers some fine seascapes and sheltered beaches, as well as 17th-century timber-framed houses.

Returning to La Baule take the N171 past St-Nazaire, a ship-building centre and commercial port, which was practically destroyed in the last war. Although it has made a remarkable recovery there is little of interest here for the tourist, beyond the harbour (former submarine base) and the Monument to the Commandos, commemorating the 1942 Anglo–Canadian Raid. Instead continue on the N171/165 to Nantes, situated either side of the Loire, where the Erdre and Sèvre meet. Nantes was once Brittany's largest city, and is now a great metropolis of France.

Nantes

Much of Nantes' history is Brittany's too. It was here in 939 that Alain Barbe-Torte, returned from England to rout the Normans below Nantes and drive them out of Brittany. He became Duke, rebuilt Nantes and made it his capital. It was several times Brittany's capital during the Middle Ages. In 1434 Duc Jean V started to build the cathedral; in 1465 Duc François II started to rebuild the 13th-century castle and founded the University of Nantes. His daughter, the Duchess Anne, also governed from Nantes. By the end of the

18th century, Nantes was one of the most important ports in France. Proud mansions, built by shipowners, still line the Quai-de-la-Fosse and the old island of Feydeau. When the river silted up gradually, preventing large ships from using the port, Nantes turned to industry. An urban renewal plan (begun in 1920) and rebuilding due to the destruction caused by the Germans in the last war, has extended and changed the old city. The port has been rebuilt and the arms of rivers filled in and made into roads. But, in spite of the wide boulevards and parks, something of old Brittany still remains. A maze of old streets lie on the east side of the curving Cours de 50 Otages (runs above last stretch of river Erdre). The newer classical Nantes is on the west side.

Two buildings here you should not miss are the cathedral and castle.

The cathedral St Peter and St Paul (built between 1434 and 1893), has an imposing facade, and a particularly fine interior. White stone has been used instead of the usual Breton granite and the vaulting reaches a height of 120 feet. The cathedral's most important objet d'art is the Renaissance tomb of François II, commissioned by Anne of Brittany to receive the remains of her father and mother (Anne of Foix) by Michel Colombe. The casket, which once contained the heart of the Duchess Anne, is now in the Dobrée museum.

If you walk down Rue Mathelin-Rodier, you will arrive at the Château of the Dukes. Duchess Anne continued her father's work of construction. Later defences were added by the Duke of Mercoeur, and the castle was taken over by the military in the 18th century, who added some parts and destroyed others. In 1915, the city of Nantes restored it as best they could, and have added three museums — one of folklore and popular Breton art; one of more modern textile and decorative arts; and one depicting seafaring Nantes of the 18th century.

Joustings and tournaments took place, and plays were performed in the large courtyard. Note the beautiful well, whose wrought-iron framework (once gilded) represents the ducal crown. Behind the well is the governor's palace (rebuilt after a fire in 1684), and next to it the Grand Logis, where the men-of-arms once lived. The castle has some interesting towers — Fouquet of Belle Île stayed in one before he was seized by Louis XIV's men. Many French kings visited Nantes' castle, but its golden age was during the time of François II.

During the Revolution, its overcrowded prisons and towers housed priests,

Vendéens, Royalists and suspects. The notorious Carrier sent by the Convention in Paris to purge the town of 'rotten matter' decided to empty the prisons by drowning all the inmates in the Loire. Condemned prisoners were put in barges, which were scuttled in the Loire opposite Chantenay.

If you want a rest from sightseeing, there is a pleasant park, the Jardin des Plantes, formally laid out, but with pools, pretty waterfalls, trees and exotic plants, not far from the castle. Walk down Rue de Richbourg and cross Rue Stanislas Boudry. The Fine Arts museum lies in nearby Rue Georges Clemenceau (works range from primitives to moderns). On the other side of the centre, the Palais Dobrée, in Rue Dobrée, and 15th-century Manoir du Jean V, once country house of the Bishops of Nantes, next door, are both museums and include relics of the Vendéen war.

Continue down to the waterfront and west to the Quai d'Aiguillon for the Musée Jules Verne, where there is a permanent exhibition of the works and memorabilia of Nantes' greatest author.

Dinner and overnight at Les Trois Marchands, Nantes.

Restaurant L'Espadon
2 Avenue de la Plage
44503 La Baule
Tel: 40 60 05 63

The restaurant and terrace overlook the magnificent white sandy beach and the rest of the resort.

Closed:	January, and Sunday evenings and Mondays
Credit cards:	Visa, American Express, Diners Club
Food:	Ballotine de lotte aux morilles, Huître de fines de claires à l'emincée de saumon fumé are good examples of the imaginative menus.
Rating:	★★★★

```
┌─────────────────────────────────────────────────────────┐
│  USEFUL INFORMATION: LA BAULE                            │
│  Tourist Office:        Place Victoire                   │
│                         Tel: 40 24 34 44                 │
│  Population:            14,688                           │
│  Amenities:             Casino, golf                     │
└─────────────────────────────────────────────────────────┘
```

Hôtel Restaurant Les Trois Marchands
26 Rue Armand Brossard
44000 Nantes
Tel: 40 47 62 00

Situated in a quiet street in the centre of Nantes.

Open:	All year
Rooms:	64
Facilities:	Restaurant, car park
Credit cards:	Carte Bleu, American Express, Diners Club, Visa
Food:	In keeping with the traditional style of the hotel the food is simple and good value.
Rating:	★★★

```
┌─────────────────────────────────────────────────────────┐
│  USEFUL INFORMATION: NANTES                              │
│  Tourist Office:        Place Commerce                   │
│                         Tel: 40 47 04 51                 │
│  Population:            247, 227                         │
│  Amenities:             Golf, small airfield             │
└─────────────────────────────────────────────────────────┘
```

Vitré

DAY 10

Nantes to Rennes: approx 75 miles.

Today begins the journey back to St-Malo. After a morning's sightseeing in Nantes we travel north, via Châteaubriant for lunch, to Rennes for the afternoon. Rennes is Brittany's capital and combines both classical 18th-century architecture with the attractions of an old quarter where the maze of narrow streets is lined with 15th-century houses with overhanging storeys.

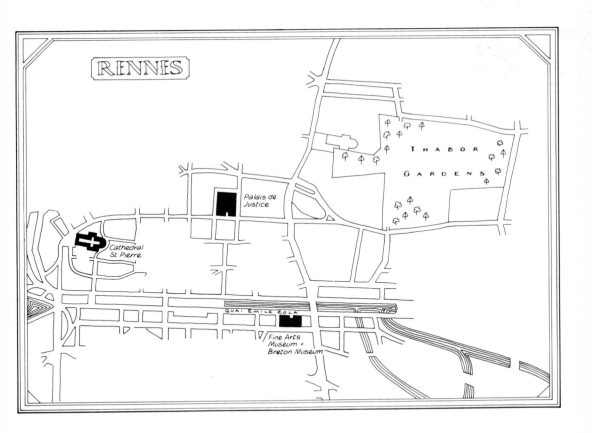

Travels in Brittany

Breakfast at Nantes.

After further sightseeing in Nantes you may wish to lunch at Nantes before starting the journey northwards. Alternatively, leave Nantes late morning by the D178.

Châteaubriant

The castle at Châteaubriant dominates the town both physically and historically. Physically, the castle is a rather fine, primarily Renaissance, building which has retained the medieval square keep. Historically the associations are sad. Firstly there was the faithful lady Sybille, who died of joy when she embraced her husband when he returned from a Crusade in 1250. Secondly, there was the 16th-century Françoise de Foix who was married when eleven to the jealous Jean de Laval, Count of Châteaubriant, who tried to hide her away, thus incurring great curiosity, especially from the King, François I. The king tricked him into bringing the innocent girl to court and she subsequently became the king's mistress. When she was superseded by the Duchess of Étampes, her husband took her back to Châteaubriant and shut her away with her seven-year-old daughter in a room hung with black. The child died but the mother lingered on for ten years until, it is said, her jealous husband killed her with his sword.

The third sad story is that of the hostages held here in 1941 against the local Resistance's good behaviour. When in October a German colonel was killed in ambush, hostages — the youngest was 16 — were shot here while others were taken to Nantes and shot. There is a memorial to this event at the Carrière des Fusilles at the town gates on the road to Pouance.

Lunch at le Poêlon d'Or, Châteaubriant.

Follow the D163 to Rennes.

Detour

Instead of going direct to Rennes take D178 to Vitré, an old border town on the frontier of France. This is one of the best-preserved of Brittany's medieval towns; its remaining ramparts and network of old streets are much as they were so many centuries ago.

The town is built on a spur overlooking the deep Vilaine valley with its castle perched commandingly above. The best view of this ensemble is from the bridge over the river.

From the 16th to the 18th century, Vitré was one of Brittany's most prosperous cities. It sold hemp, woollen cloth and cotton stockings in many parts of Europe and even as far afield as America. Trade declined in the 19th century but has revived again in this. Boots and shoes, knitted goods, agricultural machinery and furniture are just a few of the products made and sold here today.

The castle which follows the contours of the rock on which it stands is somewhat triangular in shape. It was rebuilt in the 13th, 14th and 15th centuries on the foundations of an older building and belonged in turn to the lords of Montfort, Rieux, Coligny and Trémoille. Like all such frontier strongholds it underwent numerous sieges — in the Hundred Years' War, in the Wars of Religion and by the Duke of Mercoeur. It was bought by the town from the Trémoille family in 1820 and has been restored. Inside is a good museum in St-Laurent tower (folklore, excavation of the neighbourhood and audio-visual display of the architecture of Vitré through the centuries); in the Argentan tower there is a section on Natural History. The 17th-century Marquise de Sévigné, renowned for her letter-writing, lived for 20 years at the nearby Château au Rochers-Sévigné. Only part of it is open to the public. Take the D857/N157 to Rennes.

Ille-et-Vilaine

Dignified Rennes, strategically sited at the confluence of the Vilaine and Ille rivers, is Brittany's capital and gateway. It is a booming modern town surrounded by sprawling suburbs and industrial zones (car manufacture, railway equipment, etc.) and a centre for the electronics and communications industry. As a university city it has a large student population.

In early times, it was known as Condate, the oppidum of the Redons' tribe. Under Roman occupation, it became an important communications centre and market town, and its history was similar to that of other frontier towns. In 1213, when Upper and Lower Brittany were united, it was proclaimed capital of Brittany, whose dukes came here to claim their crowns. The parliament of Brittany was established here in 1560, but in 1675, after an insurrection against the tobacco and stamp duties, parliament was transferred to Vannes for a while.

Rennes great disaster came on 22 December, 1720, when a drunken carpenter set fire to some shavings with his lamp, setting alight the building, which ignited others. The resulting conflagration lasted a week, and destroyed a large part of the town. It was rebuilt by Jacques Gabriel in the new 'classical' style — rectangular, uniform streets lined by tall, severely-distinguished granite houses, more French than Breton, at the crown's expense.

Although the Rennes' parliament often opposed the decrees of the constituent assembly of the French Revolution, it eventually became the headquarters of the Republican army during their fight against the Vendéens.

In spite of the fire and the last war's destruction, there is still a little bit of old Rennes to see — a maze of 15th- to 16th-century houses with overhanging storeys and mansions of sculptured facades. The 'king' and 'queen' of Brittany once rode through the old gate, 'Porte Mordelaise', to the cathedral, where they were crowned. St-Pierre, completed in 1844 (three churches have stood on this site since the 6th century) has a rich interior, incorporating a variety of styles. Note the 15th-century gilded and carved wood altarpiece in the chapel before the main transept.

Rennes' most imposing building is the Palais de Justice. Its first floor holds some magnificent rooms, decorated by painters such as Jouvenet and Coypel, the most impressive being the Grand' Chambre, with its panelled ceiling, rich woodwork and ten modern Gobelins' tapestries (depicting episodes from Brittany's historic past). This was Rennes' former parliamentary debating chamber. Distinguished visitors could listen to debates from the finely-decorated loggias.

While in Rennes, you should visit the Thabor gardens (incorporates rose, botanical and French classical gardens), reckoned to be one of the best public gardens in France. It was once owned by the Bénédictine abbey, St-Melaine (Melaine, an adviser to Clovis, was a famous healer). Rennes also has some good museums. The Fine Arts museum (French and foreign schools from 16th century), and the Breton museum (a folklore museum) are conveniently situated together in one building on Quai Emile-Zola.

Detour

West of Rennes lies the forest of Paimpont (N24) the ancient Broceliande, where according to legend, the sorcerer Merlin met the fairy Viviane, who enclosed him, not too unwillingly, in a magic circle from which he could not escape. Paimpont forest which now covers an area of 27 sq. miles is all that remains in the east of the great forest which once covered a large part of inner Brittany. Trees cut down to fuel the forges was a main factor in its deforestation. Conifers have been replanted over the last few years. Many pretty corners remain; woods, heathland and tangles of undergrowth, streams and ponds, added to the many Arthurian legends, make it an attractive area to ramble through.

Dinner and overnight at Hôtel Sévigné, Rennes.

Le Poêlon d'Or
30 rue du 11 Novembre
Châteaubriant
Tel: 40 81 43 33

Situated right in the centre of town this establishment offers good food at reasonable prices.

Closed:	21 August to 28 December, Saturday midday and Sunday evenings
Credit cards:	American Express, Diners, Visa
Rating:	★★

USEFUL INFORMATION: CHÂTEAUBRIANT

Tourist Office:	40 Rue Château Tel: 40 81 04 53
Population:	14,415

Hôtel Sévigné
47 avenue Janvier
Rennes
Tel: 99 67 27 55

Open all year	
Rooms:	48
Credit cards:	American Express, Diners, Eurocard, Visa
Rating:	★★★

Hôtel du Guesclin et restaurant Goéland
5 rue Gare
Rennes
Tel: 99 31 47 47

Open all year
Rooms:	68
Credit cards:	American Express, Visa, Diners, Eurocard
Rating:	★★★

For gourmet food try:

Le Palais
7 place Parlement de Bretagne
Rennes
Tel: 99 79 45 01

Closed:	8 to 31 August, February and Sunday evening and Mondays
Credit cards:	American Express, Diners, Visa, Eurocard
Rating:	★★★

Le Corsaire
52 rue Antrain
Rennes
Tel: 99 36 33 69

Closed:	2 to 25 August and Sundays
Credit cards:	American Express, Diners, Visa, Eurocard
Rating:	★★★

USEFUL INFORMATION: RENNES

Tourist Office:	Pont de Nemours
	Tel: 99 79 01 98
Population:	200,390
Amenities:	Golf, small airfield

DAY 11 — POSTSCRIPT

Rennes to St-Malo: approx. 85 miles.

The journey north continues and obviously the time at your disposal depends on your sailing time. From Rennes the most direct route takes you to the romantic fortress at Combourg and on by the prehistoric mound at Dol — where the devil fought St Michel and lost. From Dol the route skirts the bay of Mont-St-Michel and crosses over to St-Malo.

Travels in Brittany

Breakfast at Rennes.

Depending upon your sailing time from St-Malo you can either drive directly north to Combourg (N137/D795) or take a more indirect route via Fougères detailed below.

Detour

Take to D12 to Fougères.

Fougères, predominantly an industrial town and a traditional centre for shoe manufacture, is pictorially sited overlooking the Nanson valley. Its massive 13th-century fortress, surrounded by water, stands below on the valley floor. The best view of the castle with its 13 towers, is from the Place aux Arbres, a public garden partly situated in the town's ramparts. Described by Victor Hugo as the Carcassonne of the north it was once one of the most impressive medieval fortresses in France and has a history as romantic as its appearance. Despite its hugeness, it has often been captured. Henry II of England, St Louis, du Guesclin, the Duke of Mercoeur, and the Vendéen army are just a few who fought their way in. Governors lived here when Brittany was united with France and ten of the towers bear their names. One tower was added by the Lusignan family, who claimed descent from the fairy Mélusine, and so the tower is named after her. The castle was bought by the town at the end of the 19th century.

A visit to the castle takes about an hour. You can walk round the ramparts and tour the inside. The gothic church St-Sulpice in the town is also worth seeing. Balzac described the town in the book *Les Chouans*. Follow the D155 to Dol.

Combourg

Combourg, another castle town, is set beside a lake, with its feudal fortress (11th-, 14th- and 15th-century) romantically towering above. It once belonged to the du Guesclin family, and later, in the 18th century, to the Count of Chateaubriand, father of the Breton writer, François-René de Chateaubriand (1768–1848). The gloomy haunted castle is mentioned in the author's book, *Mémoires d'Outre-Tombe* (Memoirs from Beyond the Tomb). You can visit his room in the Cat Tower — haunted by a cat, supposed to be inhabited by the spirit of a former lord of Combourg — which along with another room, has been made into a museum. Nearby is the ruined medieval castle of Montmuran (part is open to the public, and it has a small museum) and a very pretty church (15th- to 16th-century) contains some remarkable 16th-century stained-glass windows, at Les Iffs.

Lunch at Combourg at the Hôtel du Château.

Dol, (D795 to the north of Combourg) seems to be comprised of one long street — Grande-Rue-des-Stuarts — which contains several handsome old houses, including the 12th-century Maison des Plaids and the 15th-century Maison de la Guillotière (now a museum). Various steep side streets run off it to lead up to its vast, granite, 13th- to 16th-century cathedral, St-Samson, founded by a monk, Samson, who died about 565. Its towers and turrets put one in mind more of a Norman fortress than a church. It was rebuilt by King John as an act of reparation — he had burned down the earlier one. Note the witty, 14th-century choir stalls inside.

Dol, situated on the frontier between Normandy and Brittany, was often attacked by the Normans — William the Conqueror (he was defeated in 1076), Henry II and John are three Norman dukes and English kings who laid seige to the town. It was at Dol, also, that the Vendéens obtained a great victory, after a bloody battle in 1793. In 1795, their last bishop, M. Hercé, was shot along with other Royalist supporters at Vannes after the failure of the Quiberon landings.

Behind the cathedral lies the Promenade des Douves, from which there is a grand view of the Marais, the drained salty marshland, which stretches towards the coast and Mont-St-Michel. The Dol mound, 275 feet high, contains the remains of many prehistoric animals, and is the site of a legendary struggle between the devil and St Michel. (St Michel won and dashed back to his Mont.) The chapel, Notre-Dame-de-l'Espérance, is the goal of a popular pilgrimage to the mound. A mile south of Dol stands one of Brittany's finest menhirs.

From Dol the D155 skirts Mont-St-Michel Bay and crosses inland to St-Malo and your ferry home.

Hôtel du Château
1 Place Châteaubriand
35270 Combourg
Tel: 99 73 00 38

Suitably elegant dining room but good value fixed price menus.

Closed:	15 December to 25 January
Rooms:	33
Credit cards:	Carte Bleu, Diners Club, American Express, Access
Food:	Interesting and varied with a distinctly regional slant.
Rating:	★★

USEFUL INFORMATION: COMBOURG

Tourist Office:	Maison de la Lanterne
	Tel: 99 73 13 93
Population:	4,763

Recipes
from the Region

MENU 1 ❦

Maquereaux à la façon de Quimper
Mackerel as prepared in Quimper

. . .

Caneton nantais
Duck with peas
Steamed new potatoes

. . .

Crémet nantais aux fraises
Cream cheese with strawberries

. . .

*Wine suggestion
A Bordeaux from Canon-Fronsac or the
Côtes de Bourg

* In the menus that follow we suggest a range of wines to accompany the meals, however this is only done in deference to common practice. In Brittany cider or the local wine is the most likely accompaniment.

Maquereaux à la façon de Quimper
Mackerel as prepared in Quimper

2 good-sized mackerel
2 egg yolks
1 tbs Dijon mustard
1 tsp wine vinegar
2–3 tbs chopped fresh
herbs — chervil, chives,
parsley, tarragon
salt and pepper
2 oz/50 g butter
parsley sprigs

For the court-bouillon
1 pint/600 ml water
½ pint/300 ml dry cider
or white wine
1 tbs cider or wine
vinegar
2 carrots, sliced
2 large onions, sliced
1 tsp black peppercorns,
crushed
2 tarragon sprigs
salt

Serves 4

Make the court-bouillon by simmering all the ingredients together for 30 minutes. Leave to cool. Put the mackerel into a pan and strain over the lukewarm court-bouillon. Bring it slowly to the boil, then simmer gently until the mackerel are cooked — about 8–10 minutes. Remove the fish from the liquid, let them cool, then skin and fillet them.

Put the egg yolks into a bowl and stir in the mustard. Add the vinegar, herbs, salt and pepper and stir well. Melt the butter and pour it, lukewarm, into the sauce, stirring all the time. The sauce should have the consistency of a light mayonnaise.

Arrange the mackerel fillets around a serving dish with the sauce in the middle. Garnish it with sprigs of parsley.

Caneton nantais
Duck with peas

1 duck weighing 6 lb/
3 kg
sprig thyme
bay leaf
2 oz/50 g butter
2 tbs ground nut oil

Season the duck with salt and pepper, put a sprig of thyme, the bay leaf and a knob of butter into the cavity. Heat the remaining butter and the oil in a heavy casserole and brown the duck on all sides. Remove it from the pan and keep warm.

4 lb/2 kg fresh peas,
shelled
1 carrot, sliced
4 oz/100 g smoked
streaky bacon, cut into
small pieces
12 tiny onions
1 sugar lump
2 sprigs savory
¼ pint/150 ml Muscadet
or other dry white wine
¼ pint/150 ml stock or
water
salt and pepper

Serves 4

Drain off any excess fat, there should be 2–3 tbs left in the pan. Put in the peas, carrot, bacon and onions, and if you have them, the heart and liver of the duck. Sauté for a few minutes, until the onions start to look transparent, then season with salt and pepper and add the sugar lump and the sprigs of savory. Pour over the wine and stock. Put the duck in the middle of the vegetables and baste with some of the liquid.

Bring the pan to the boil, then cover it and transfer it to a preheated oven 170°C/325°F/gas 3. Cook until the duck is done, about 1 hour.

Remove the duck from the pan and keep warm. Reduce the liquid left in the pan with the vegetables, stirring so that the vegetables do not stick. When there are only a few tablespoons remaining, remove the savory and put the vegetables around the duck on a hot serving dish.

Crémet nantais aux fraises
Cream cheese with strawberries

1 lb/500 g strawberries
¾ lb/375 g crémet
nantais or similar light
cream cheese
caster sugar

Serves 4

Rinse, dry and hull the strawberries. Arrange the cheese on four plates, surrounded by the strawberries and hand the sugar separately.

133

```
┌─────────────────────────────────────────────────┐
│                                                 │
│   MENU 2 ❧                                       │
│                                                 │
│                  Cotriade                        │
│            Fish broth followed by                │
│             fish and potatoes                    │
│                                                 │
│                                                 │
│                 .  .  .                          │
│                                                 │
│                Green salad                       │
│                                                 │
│                 .  .  .                          │
│                                                 │
│                                                 │
│              Gâteau Breton                       │
│               Breton cake                        │
│                                                 │
│                 .  .  .                          │
│                                                 │
│                                                 │
│               Wine suggestion                    │
│          A robust red e.g. Cahors.               │
│                                                 │
└─────────────────────────────────────────────────┘
```

Cotriade

2 gurnard
2 whiting
1 piece conger eel,
skinned and sliced
1 lb/500 g cod or
hake fillet

Cut the fish into large pieces. Heat the butter in a big pan and sauté the onions, shallots and garlic until translucent. Add 2½ pints/1.5 litres cold water, the potatoes, thyme, bay leaf, parsley and seasoning and cook for 15–20 minutes, until the potatoes are nearly done.

2 mackerel
3–4 fresh sardines
3 oz/75 g butter
3 onions, sliced
2 shallots, sliced
3 cloves garlic, chopped
2 lb/1 kg potatoes,
quartered
2 sprigs thyme
bay leaf
large handful chopped
parsley
salt and pepper
6–8 slices day-old bread

Serves 6–8

Add the fish and cook for a further 10 minutes. When the fish is ready, check the seasoning, then lift out the fish and potatoes and keep warm.

The broth is served first as a soup, ladled over the slices of bread. Then the fish and potatoes are served with lots of salty butter or a vinaigrette dressing.

Gâteau Breton
Breton Cake

5 oz/150 g salted butter,
melted
5 oz/150 g sugar
5 oz/150 g flour
4 eggs
1 teaspoon orange
flower water
½ oz/10 g fresh yeast or
¼ oz/5 g dried yeast
creamed in a little warm
milk

Serves 6–8

Mix well together the butter, sugar and flour. Separate the eggs and add the yolks and the orange flower water and yeast to the mixture. Cover the bowl and leave to stand in a warm place for an hour.

Preheat the oven to 190°C/375°F/gas 5. Butter an 8 in/20 cm shallow (2 in/5 cm high) cake tin. Beat the egg whites to a firm snow and fold into the cake batter. Pour the batter into the tin and bake for 40 minutes, without opening the door.

Allow the cake to cool in the tin for a few minutes, then remove and transfer to a wire rack.

135

MENU 3 ❦

Palourdes Farcies
Stuffed clams

. . .

Gigot à la Bretonne
Leg of lamb with haricot beans

. . .

Paris-Brest
Praline filled pastry

. . .

Wine suggestion
A red Rhône e.g. Vacqueras or Gigondas

Palourdes Farcies
Stuffed clams

3 dozen clams
2 shallots, finely
chopped
2 garlic cloves, finely
chopped
6 oz/175 g salted butter,
softened and cut in
pieces
2 tbs chopped parsley
salt and pepper
3–4 tbs Muscadet or
other dry white wine

Serves 6

Put the shallots, garlic, butter, parsley, a pinch of salt and a good grinding of pepper into the liquidizer or food processor and blend. Towards the end add the wine through the feed tube and when it is absorbed, the 'stuffing' is ready. If you do not have a machine to do the job for you, pound the garlic and shallots in a mortar, then add the butter, parsley and seasonings and finally the wine.

Open the clams with a knife, or if you prefer, steam them open. Leave them on the half shell and drain off any liquid. Coat the clams with the butter mixture and put them in a hot oven — 220°C/425°F/gas 7 for 8–10 minutes. Serve as soon as the butter is bubbling.

Gigot à la Bretonne
Leg of lamb with haricot beans

1 leg of lamb weighing
5–6 lb/2.5–3 kg
2 cloves garlic
salt, pepper
thyme
2 oz/50 g butter
2 onions
2 carrots
¼ pint/150 ml stock or
water

Start by preparing the beans. Put them into a large pan with the onion, carrot, celery and bouquet garni. Cover with water, bring to the boil and simmer for 1–2 hours (it is difficult to give a more precise time, since all depends on the age of the beans) or until cooked. If they are ready ahead of time, it doesn't matter because they reheat well.

When the beans are tender, drain them, reserving the liquid. Take out the carrot, celery and the bouquet garni, throw them away. Season the beans with salt and pepper.

137

For the beans
1½ lb/750 g white
haricot beans, soaked
for 3–4 hours
1 large onion, stuck
with a clove
1 carrot
1 stalk celery
bouquet garni
3 shallots, finely
chopped
2–3 tomatoes, peeled
and chopped
salt and pepper

Serves 6–8

Heat the butter in a pan and sauté the shallots. Chop the onion and add it together with the tomatoes.

Season well. Cook for 2–3 minutes, then add enough of the bean liquid to make a thin sauce. Reheat the beans gently in the sauce while the meat is standing.

To roast the lamb, preheat the oven to 230°C/ 450°F/gas 8. Peel the garlic cloves, cut them in half; make incisions in the meat and push the pieces of garlic in near the bone. Season the lamb with salt, pepper and powdered dried thyme, rub all over with half the butter.

Peel and slice the onions and carrots, melt the rest of the butter in your roasting tin and spread the vegetables over the bottom. Season them too with salt, pepper and thyme. Put the leg of lamb on the vegetables and sear the meat for 10 minutes, turning it once.

Lower the heat to 190°C/380°F/gas 5 and pour in a little of the stock. Roast the leg for 10 minutes per 1 lb/500 g for rare meat, 15 minutes per 1 lb/500 g for medium. Baste frequently. Let the lamb stand in a warm place for 15 minutes before carving.

Skim the excess fat from the tin, pour in the remaining stock and deglaze over high heat. Strain the gravy into a sauce boat, pushing the vegetables well against the sieve to give the gravy some body.

Serve the lamb on a hot dish. The beans may be spooned around it or served separately.

Paris-Brest

For the choux pastry
8 fl oz/250 ml water
1 tbs caster sugar
pinch of salt
2½ oz/65 g butter
5 oz/150 g plain flour
4 eggs

For the filling
1 egg
2 oz/50 g almonds, flaked
½ pint/300 ml double cream, whipped
3 oz/75 g praline powder (see below)
icing sugar

Serves 6

Preheat the oven to 180°C/350°F/gas 4. To make the choux pastry, put the water, sugar, salt and butter into a large pan. Heat gently until the butter has melted, then bring to the boil. As the liquid boils, remove the pan from the heat and tip in all of the flour. Beat furiously until smooth, then return the pan to the heat for a minute.

When the dough comes away from the sides of pan, remove the pan from the heat again and beat in the eggs, one by one. The dough should be shiny and soft enough to fall from the spoon. Put the dough into a pastry bag with a ¾ in/2 cm plain nozzle. Grease a baking tray and on it pipe a circle of choux paste about the size of the rim of a dinner plate. (You can line the tray with greased paper and draw round a dinner plate on the paper if you wish.)

Beat 1 egg and brush the pastry circle, then sprinkle with almonds and bake for 20–25 minutes. Remove from the oven and slice across in two while it is still warm. Leave to cool. Just before serving the cake, flavour the whipped cream with praline powder, and sandwich the cake together with the cream. Sprinkle icing sugar all over the top and serve.

To make praline powder
8 oz/250 g sugar
4 tbs water
8 oz/250 g almonds

Make a thick syrup with the sugar and water. Add the almonds and cook gently until the mixture is toffee-coloured. Pour it out onto an oiled marble or formica surface and leave to get cold. When it is quite cold it will be very hard. Break into pieces and grind to a powder in a food processor, blender or electric coffee grinder.

MENU 4 ✤❀✤

Galettes de Blé Noir aux Oignons
Buckwheat pancakes with onions

.   .   .

Lotte à la Bretonne
Monkfish in cream sauce
Boiled potatoes

.   .   .

Far

.   .   .

Wine suggestion
White Sancerre or Muscadet

Galettes de Blé Noir aux Oignons
Buckwheat pancakes with onions

10 oz/300 g buckwheat flour
salt and pepper
4 eggs
½ pint/300 ml dry cider
¾ pint/450 ml water (approx)
6 oz/175 g salted butter
2 lb/1 kg onions, thinly sliced

Serves 6

Combine the flour and a pinch of salt in a large bowl. Make a well in the centre and add the eggs, one at a time, beating each one in. Thin the mixture by pouring in the cider in a trickle, beating well all the time. Then add enough water to make a thick, smooth batter. Melt 2 oz/50 g butter and stir it into the batter. Now leave the batter to rest at room temperature for at least an hour, and preferably longer.

An hour or so before you are ready to make the pancakes, cook the onions. Melt 2 oz/50 g butter in a large heavy casserole, put in the onions and stir through the butter. Cover the pan and put it on the lowest possible heat for 45 minutes to an hour. Stir it occasionally. The onions must not brown or fry, but should slowly melt in the butter until they are soft and golden. Leave them in the covered pan to keep warm while you make the pancakes.

To cook the pancakes, heat a griddle or a heavy frying pan, grease it with a little butter and pour in a ladleful of the batter. Spread it out well to cover the surface and cook over high heat for 2 minutes. Turn the pancake with a spatula and spread a little butter over the top. Spread some of the onion mixture on half of the pancake and fold it in half. Butter the top lightly and cook for a minute. Fold the pancake into quarters, transfer it to a dish in a warm oven and keep hot while you make the others. Don't forget to butter the griddle each time.

141

Lotte à la Bretonne
Monkfish in cream sauce

3 lb/1.5 kg monkfish
6 shallots, chopped
3 carrots, sliced
1 lb/500 g celeriac,
cubed
3 oz/75 g butter
small glass dry white
wine
½ pint/300 ml court-
bouillon, made with
wine (see p. 132)
¼ pint/150 ml crème
fraîche
salt and pepper

Serves 6

Remove the monkfish bone and the thin greyish membrane and cut the fish into chunks. Sauté the shallots, carrots and celeriac gently in the butter for 15–20 minutes or until they become soft. Put the vegetables, together with the fish, into an ovenproof dish, such as a gratin dish. Season with salt and pepper.

Deglaze the vegetable pan with the white wine, then add the court-bouillon, let it boil steadily for about 10 minutes, until reduced by half. Pour half of the court-bouillon over the fish and vegetables and put the dish into a preheated oven, 190°C/375°F/gas 5, for 25 minutes. Baste from time to time.

When the fish and vegetables are almost cooked beat the crème fraîche into the remaining court-bouillon over medium heat. Check the seasoning and pour the sauce over the dish just before serving.

Far

3 eggs
3 oz/75 g sugar
5 oz/150 g plain flour
pinch of salt
¾ pint/450 ml milk
1 oz/25 g butter

Preheat the oven to 200°C/400°F/gas 6. Beat well together — in a food processor or a blender if you wish — the eggs, sugar, flour and salt. Pour in the milk, a little at a time, blending or beating until you have a smooth batter.

4 oz/125 g dried apricots, soaked in a little rum or eau-de-vie (optional)

Serves 6

Well butter an earthenware oven dish. Add the soaked apricots to the mixture if you are using them, and pour it into the dish. Bake for about 30 minutes, or until the far is set, turning the oven down to 180°C/360°F/gas 4 after 15 minutes. Let the far cool before serving.

Note: prunes, first soaked in water for several hours and then stoned, make a good alternative to the apricots.

MENU 5 ✤

Artichauts Vinaigrette
Artichokes vinaigrette

. . .

Poisson au Beurre Blanc
Fish with white butter sauce
New potatoes and spinach/carrots

. . .

Crêpes de Froment au Miel
Pancakes with honey

. . .

Wine suggestion
Muscadet

Artichauts vinaigrette
Artichokes vinaigrette

6 large artichokes
salt and pepper
8 tbs wine or cider
vinegar
1 tbs Dijon mustard
8 tbs olive oil

Serves 6

Break the stalks off the artichokes, pulling away
any strings. Remove any discoloured or damaged
leaves. Soak the artichokes for 30 minutes or so
in salted water to get rid of any dirt or insects
that might be hidden in the leaves.

Put 4 tbs vinegar and some salt into a large pan
of water and bring to the boil. Put in the
artichokes, bring back to the boil and cook for
30 minutes. To see if the artichokes are ready
pull a leaf from the base of one. If it comes out
easily, they are ready.

Remove the artichokes and drain them upside
down in a colander.

To make the vinaigrette dissolve a pinch of salt
in the remaining vinegar, stir in mustard and
pepper, then add the oil and whisk to blend.

Serve the artichokes warm or cold with the
sauce.

For warm artichokes, melted butter and lemon
juice is a good alternative to vinaigrette.

Poisson au Beurre Blanc
Fish with white butter sauce

3 lb/1.5 kg pike, sea
bass, whiting or turbot

In southern Brittany this dish would normally be
made with a freshwater fish, such as pike, but

145

court-bouillon, made
with wine (p. 132)
6 shallots
4 tbs wine vinegar
4 tbs white wine
8 oz/250 g unsalted
butter
salt and pepper

Serves 6

pike are not easy to buy in England, so I have
suggested one or two sea fish as alternatives.

Poach the fish in the court-bouillon for 20–25
minutes if whole, about 5–8 minutes if cut into
steaks. When it is ready drain and keep warm on
a serving dish. Meanwhile, chop the shallots
finely, put them in a pan with the vinegar, wine
and 4 tbs court-bouillon, then boil over
moderate heat to reduce by two-thirds. Reduce
the heat to very low. Cut the butter into small
pieces and add, a little at a time, whisking hard.
If the butter seems to be melting, remove the
pan from the heat. The sauce should whiten and
have the consistency of thick cream. When all the
butter is incorporated, season with salt and
pepper and serve with the fish.

Crêpes de Froment au Miel
Pancakes with honey

7 oz/200 g plain flour
pinch of salt
2 eggs
¾ pint/450 ml milk
4 oz/125 g butter
6 oz/175 g runny honey

Serves 6

Sift the flour and sugar into a bowl, make a well
in the centre and add the eggs, one at a time,
beating well. Pour the milk in slowly, still
beating, until you have a smooth, thickish batter.
Melt 2 oz/50 g butter, pour it in and stir again.

Leave the batter to stand for at least an hour,
and preferably longer. Just before cooking the
pancakes, heat the honey gently and keep warm.

To cook the pancakes, melt a little butter in a
frying pan. Pour in a ladle of batter, tilt the pan
to spread it evenly and cook for about 2
minutes, until the underside is golden brown.

Turn the pancake with a spatula and cook the other side.

Slide the pancake onto a plate and brush it with honey. Roll it up and put in a serving dish in a warm oven while the other pancakes are made. More, warmed honey may be served with the pancakes if you wish.

Glossary of Food Terms

Starters

charcuterie	cold meats (pork)
crudités	raw vegetables
escargots	snails
potage	soup
terrine	a type of coarse pâté

Meats (Viande)

agneau (gigot de)	lamb (leg of)
boeuf (filet de)	beef (fillet steak)
bleu	very rare
saignant	rare
à point	medium
bien cuit	well done
brochette	kebab
côte/côtelette	chop
entrecôte	steak (rib)
jambon	ham
lapin	rabbit
lièvre	hare
mouton	mutton
saucisse	sausage (fresh)
saucisson	sausage (dry)
veau	veal

Offal (Abats)

boudin	black pudding
cervelle	brains
foie	liver
langue	tongue
ris	sweetbreads
rognon	kidney

Poultry (Volaille) and Game (Gibier)

caille	quail
canard/caneton	duck/duckling

148

coq	cockerel
faisan	pheasant
oie	goose
perdrix	partridge
pintade	guinea fowl
poulet	chicken
sanglier	wild boar

Fish (Poisson) and Shellfish (Crustacés/Coquillages)

alose	shad
anguilles (en gelée)	eels (jellied)
bouquet	prawn
brochet	pike
cabillaud	cod
coquilles St. Jacques	scallops
crevettes	prawns/shrimps
écrevisse	crayfish
fruits de mer	mixed shellfish
hareng	herring
homard	lobster
huitres	oyster
langoustine	scampi
lamproie	lamphrey
lotte	monkfish
loup de mer	sea bass
maquereau	mackerel
moules	mussels
saumon	salmon
truite	trout

Vegetables (Légumes)

ail	garlic
artichaut	artichoke (globe)
asperge	asparagus
carotte	carrot
champignon	mushroom
chou	cabbage
choucroute	sauerkraut
choufleur	cauliflower
épinards	spinach
haricots verts	French beans
navet	turnip
oignon	onion

pomme de terre	potato
au four	baked, roast
purée	mashed
petits pois	peas
poireau	leek
poivron	green/red pepper
riz	rice

Fruit

ananas	pineapples
cassis	blackcurrant
cerise	cherry
citron	lemon
fraise	strawberry
framboise	raspberry
groseille	redcurrant
mûr	blackberry
pamplemousse	grapefruit
pêche	peach
poire	pear
pomme	apple
prune	plum

Selected Bibliography

Mariners of Brittany, Peter Anson.

The Land of Pardons, Anatole le Braz, Methuen, 1906.

Early Brittany, Nora K. Chadwicke, University of Wales Press, 1969.

The Hungry Archaeologists in France, Glyn Daniel, Faber & Faber, 1963.

Megaliths in History, Glyn Daniel, Faber & Faber, 1973.

Brittany, P. Giot, Thames & Hudson, 1960.

Plodmet — Brittany, Edgar Morin, trans. by A.M. Sheridan-Smith, Allen Lane and Penguin Press, 1971.

The Lion and the Lily, Andrew Shirley, Putnam, 1956.

Brittany, Keith Spence, Victor Gollancz.

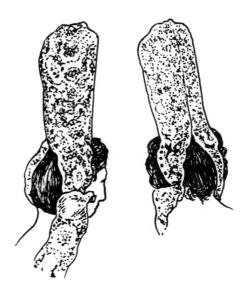

Breton coiffes

Index of Recipes

Artichauts vinaigrette 145
Galettes de Blé Noir aux Oignons 141
Maquereaux à la façon de Quimper 132
Palourdes Farcies 137

Caneton nantais 132-3
Cotriade 134-5
Gigot à la Bretonne 137-8
Lotte à la Bretonne 142
Poisson au Beure Blanc 145

Crémet nantais aux Fraises 133
Crêpes de Froment au Miel 146-7
Far 142-3
Gâteau Breton 135
Paris-Brest 139

Geographical Index

Other Merehurst Travel Titles

TRAVELS IN THE DORDOGNE
TRAVELS IN PROVENCE
TRAVELS IN TUSCANY
TRAVELS IN NORMANDY

All the titles in the series offer the reader a ten/twelve day journey
through the region pointing out places of interest, hotels and restaurants
with special emphasis on the food and wines of the area.
Each book also contains a mapped itinerary with distances and times for
each day of the journey.
As well as hints and tips on what to buy and eat in the region readers
are provided with a selection of recipes and menus which they can use on
their return to form a lasting memory of their visit.

All titles now available from bookshops or direct from Merehurst
Publishing, 5 Great James Street, London WC1N 3DA at £6.95, plus
£1.00 post and packing.

MEREHURST INTERNATIONAL TRAVEL GUIDES

INSIDER'S GUIDES offer a rare and entertaining insight into the culture and tradition of countries which are rapidly growing in popularity as holiday and business destinations. Packed with advice and information on currency, language, cuisine, and internal travel, they are all the traveller needs to make any trip a complete success.
Each complete with maps and colour illustrations.

KOREA 196 pages 200 illustrations
JAPAN 208 pages 216 illustrations
AUSTRALIA 224 pages 208 illustrations
CHINA 208 pages 208 illustrations
HONG KONG 196 pages 200 illustrations
HAWAII 224 pages 208 illustrations

All titles available from booksellers at £8.95 or direct from Merehurst Publishing at £8.95 plus £1.00 post and packing.

SETTING UP IN FRANCE

For everyone who is interested in buying, leasing, renting or time-sharing in France.

This book will cover everything from raising the money to installing water, gas, electricity, planning permissions and much more in urban and rural sites throughout France.

Written by Laetitia de Warren, the French born editor of Le Magazine, this will become 'the' reference book on the subject.

Now available from booksellers at £9.95 or direct from the publisher at £9.95 plus £1.00 post and packing.